THE MASTER BUILDER

A PLAY IN THREE ACTS

BY

HENRIK IBSEN

TRANSLATED FROM THE NORWEGIAN

BY

EDMUND GOSSE AND WILLIAM ARCHER

NEW EDITION

WITH AN INTRODUCTION BY WILLIAM ARCHER

1901

INTRODUCTION.

———•••———

Bygmester Solness, Skuespil i tre akter, was published in Christiania on December 12, and in Copenhagen on December 14, 1892. It was written in Christiania. "In the spring of 1892," says Halvorsen, "the poet was occupied in sketching out the play, and, according to his custom, crystallised in a poem the mood which then possessed him." Unlike the poems which have similarly preluded his other plays, this one has been published. It was first put on paper on March 16, 1892, and runs as follows :

DE SAD DER, DE TO.

De sad der, de to, i saa lunt et hus
ved höst og i vinterdage,
Saa brændte huset. Alt ligger i grus.
De to faar i asken rage.

For nede i den er et smykke gemt,—
et smykke, som aldrig kan brænde.
Og leder de trofast, hænder det nemt
at det findes af ham eller hende.

Men finder de end, de brandlidte to,
det dyre, ildfaste smykke,—
aldrig h u n finder sin brændte tro,
h a n aldrig sin brændte lykke.

THEY SAT THERE, THE TWO.

They sat there, the two, in so cosy a house, through autumn and winter days. Then the house burned down. Everything lies in ruins. The two must grope among the ashes.

For among them is hidden a jewel—a jewel that never can burn. And if they search faithfully, it may easily happen that he or she may find it.

But even should they find it, the burnt-out two—find this precious unburnable jewel—never will s h e find her burnt faith, h e never his burnt happiness.

It is to be hoped that the prelude-poems to Ibsen's other plays will one day be given to the world. Meanwhile this single example of the form in which a dramatic idea first presented itself to the poet's mind may perhaps help critics to recognise the absurdity of classing him as a realist.

But another of his poems, one of the earliest he ever wrote—first printed in 1858—is also, in some sort, a prelude to *The Master Builder.* It is entitled *Byggeplaner* (*Building Plans*) :

Jeg mindes saa grant, som om idag det var hændt,
den kveld jeg saa i bladet mit förste digt paa prent.
Der sad jeg paa min hybel og med dampende drag
jeg rögte og jeg drömte i salig selvbehag.

" Et skyslot vil jeg bygge. Det skal lyse over Nord.
To flöje skal der være ; en liden og en stor.
Den store skal huse en udödelig skald ;
den lille skal tjene et pigebarn til hal."

Mig syntes at i planen var en herlig harmoni ;
men siden er der kommet forstyrrelse deri.
Da mester blev fornuftig, blev slottet splittergalt :
Storflöjen blev for liden, den lille flöj forfaldt.

I remember as clearly as if it had been to-day the evening when, in the paper, I saw my first poem in print. There I sat in my den, and with long-drawn puffs I smoked and I dreamed in blissful self-complacency.

" I will build a cloud-castle. It shall shine all over the North. It shall have two wings : one little and one great. The great wing shall shelter a deathless poet ; the little wing shall serve as a young girl's bower."

The plan seemed to me nobly harmonious ; but as time went on it fell into confusion. When the master grew reasonable, the castle turned utterly crazy ; the great wing became too little, the little wing fell to ruin.[1]

Thus we see that thirty-five years before the date of *Bygmester Solness,* Ibsen's imagination was preoccupied with the symbol of a master building a castle in the air, and a young girl in one of its towers.

Germany and England were both well ahead of Scandinavia[2] in placing *The Master Builder* on the stage. It was produced at the Lessing Theater, Berlin, January 19, 1893, with Emanuel Reicher as Solness, Frl. Meyer as Mrs. Solness, and Frl. Reisenhofer as Hilda. Of this performance the critic of *Die Gegenwart* wrote :

The theatre, which exaggerates everything, certainly does nothing to diminish the obscurities of *Baumeister Solness*—least of all by means of so defective a performance. Moreover, Director Blumenthal had wielded his red pencil with such a brutal lack of comprehension that one can only counsel the poet, on another occasion, to seek the hospitality of a more sympathetic theatre. Frl. Marie Meyer alone,

---

[1] See also metrical translation in Boyesen's *Commentary on the Works of Henrik Ibsen,* p. 158.

[2] It is true that a touring company produced the play in Trondhjem on the same date (January 19, 1893) as that of its first performance in Berlin.

who played Frau Solness, was equal to the task imposed upon her. The two superhuman leading characters were quite misrepresented. Reicher was dry and affected, a weary *fin-de-siècle* personage, and Frl. Reisenhofer was an ill-mannered, hysterical schoolgirl—nothing more. In neither of them was there a spark of dæmonic fire.

The first-night reception of the performance seems to have been more than dubious. It was given only three times in all ; and other German theatres do not appear, at this time, to have attempted the play. Not till five years later (about the date of Ibsen's seventieth birthday) was it produced in Munich by the "Akademisch-Dramatische Verein," March 2, 1898, in Frankfort, March 19, 1898, and at the Burgtheater, Vienna, at the close of the same month. The following is the play-bill of the Vienna production :

K. k. HOF-BURGTHEATER

am Samstag den 26 März 1898,

zum erstenmale :

BAUMEISTER SOLNESS.

Schauspiel in drei Aufzügen von Henrik Ibsen.

Halvard Solness	Hr. ROBERT
Aline, seine Gattin . . .	Fr. MITTERWURZER
Dr. Herdal, Hausarzt . . .	Hr. RÖMPLER
Knut Brovik, Assistent bei Solness	Hr. SCHÖNE
Ragnar, sein Sohn . . .	Hr. HOFMEISTER
Kaja Fosli, Brovik's Nichte, Buchhalterin	Frl. MEDELSKY
Hilda Wangel	Fr. HOHENFELS

The Director of the Burgtheater, Dr. Paul Schlenther, threw himself with great enthusiasm into this production, which was repeated eleven times in the course of the season ; but still the *Neue Freie Presse* could find nothing more luminous to say than that "the public was confronted with a great enigma, composed of a multitude of lesser enigmas." About the same time the play formed part of an Ibsen Repertory with which a company under the direction of Herr Heine made an extensive tour in Germany.[1] In the following year (October 13, 1899) *Baumeister Solness* was performed at the Berliner Theater, Berlin, with Ludwig Stahl as Solness, and Frau Prasch-Grevenberg as Hilda. This lady is said to have made a great success in the part at Meiningen—on what occasion does not appear.

So far as one can gather, the English production of *The Master Builder* seems to have been more successful than any other—thanks, no doubt, to the masterly acting of Mr. Herbert Waring and Miss Elizabeth Robins in the leading parts. The press, as we shall see, was as hostile as ever ; but Miss Robins's Hilda was so full of magnetic vitality—what the Berlin critic would perhaps have called "dæmonic" fire—that the play had a peculiar fascination even for audiences which no doubt found its symbolism sufficiently baffling. Mr. Waring's Solness was a no less admirable performance ; the mounting was good, and the production, as a whole, thoroughly smooth and finished. None of Ibsen's plays has been seen, in England, to greater advantage. The playbill of the first performance ran as follows :

[1] See Introduction to *Ghosts* (ed. 1901), p. xv.

TRAFALGAR SQUARE THEATRE.

MATINÉES,

February 20th, 21st, 22nd, 23rd, and 24th,
at 2.30,

HENRIK IBSEN'S LATEST PLAY,

THE MASTER BUILDER.

For the first time in England.

Halvard Solness . . .	Mr. HERBERT WARING
Mrs. Solness . . .	Miss LOUISE MOODIE
Dr. Herdal	Mr. JOHN BEAUCHAMP
Knut Brovik	Mr. ATHOL FORDE
Ragnar Brovik . . .	Mr. PHILIP CUNINGHAM
Kaia Fosli	Miss MARIE LINDEN
Miss Hilda Wangel . .	Miss ELIZABETH ROBINS

Under the direction of
MR. HERBERT WARING
and
MISS ELIZABETH ROBINS.

Originally announced for five matinées (February 20–24), the play was so successful that it was given for a second series of five matinées at the Trafalgar Square—now the Duke of York's—Theatre (February 27 to March 3), and was then placed in the evening bill at the Vaudeville Theatre from March 6 to March 25. In the Vaudeville production some changes were made in the cast, Miss Elsie Chester playing Mrs. Solness, Mr. Charles Allan Dr. Herdal, and Mr. Edward Rochelle Knut Brovik. Later in the same year *The Master Builder* was acted four times at the Opera Comique Theatre, in the course of a series of twelve Ibsen performances, the other plays given being *Hedda Gabler* and *Rosmersholm.* This was the playbill of the first performance :

OPERA COMIQUE THEATRE.

On Friday and Saturday, June 2nd and 3rd, at 2.30 o'clock

THE MASTER BUILDER,

A Play in Three Acts, by HENRIK IBSEN.

Translated by Mr. Edmund Gosse and
Mr. William Archer.

Hilda Wangel . . .	Miss ELIZABETH ROBINS
Kaia Fosli	Miss MARIE LINDEN
Aline Solness . . .	Miss FRANCES IVOR
Halvard Solness . .	Mr. LEWIS WALLER
Dr. Herdal . . .	Mr. CHARLES SUGDEN
Knut Brovik . . .	Mr. LEONARD OUTRAM
Ragnar Brovik . . .	Mr. SCOTT BUIST

Act I.—The Office. Act II.—The Drawing-room.
Act III.—The Terrace.

To be followed by the Fourth Act of

HENRIK IBSEN'S

BRAND.

Translated by Professor C. H. Herford.

Brand	Mr. BERNARD GOULD
Gipsy Woman . . .	Miss FRANCES IVOR
Agnes	Miss ELIZABETH ROBINS
SCENE	BRAND'S HOME.

In the following year (November 1894) Miss Robins

produced *The Master Builder* in Manchester—"under the auspices of the Manchester Independent Theatre Committee"—with Mr. Acton Bond as Solness, Miss Alexes Leighton as Mrs. Solness, Miss Florence Farr as Kaia, and Mr. Sugden as Dr. Herdal. A very intelligent criticism of this performance, signed "O. E.," appears in *The Manchester Stage* (1880–1900), reprinted from the *Manchester Guardian.*

It was not for a moment to be expected that the London press should appreciate or even tolerate *The Master Builder.* The following are some representative selections from the critics' deliverances :

"Dense mist enshrouds characters, words, actions, and motives. . . . One may compare it to the sensations of a man who witnesses a play written, rehearsed, and acted by lunatics."

"Assuredly no one may fathom the mysteries of the play, so far as it can be called a play. . . . If it did not please, it most unquestionably puzzled."

"Here we contemplate the actions of a set of lunatics, each more hopeless than the other. . . . Platitudes and inanities. . . . The play is hopeless and indefensible."

"A feast of dull dialogue and acute dementia. . . . The most dreary and purposeless drivel we have ever heard in an English theatre. . . . A pointless, incoherent, and absolutely silly piece."

"Rigmarole of an oracle, Delphic in obscurity and Gamp-like in garrulity. . . . Pulseless and purposeless play, which has idiocy written on every lineament. . . . Three acts of gibberish."

"A distracting jumble of incoherent elements. There is no story; the characters are impossible, and the motives a nightmare of perverted finger-posts."

"Sensuality . . . irreverence . . . unwholesome . . . simply blasphemous."

"Dull, mysterious, unchaste."

"A play to which even the Young Person may be taken with no more fear of harm than a severe headache. . . . Ibsen is a master

of the chaotic and meaningless epigram. . . . Thrilling moments in
last act marred by bathos. The rest idle babble."

" Presents human life in a distorted form, and is entirely without
intelligible purpose."

"Same old dulness prevails as was the feature of his previous
prosy pratings."

" The blunder has been made. *Master Builder Solness* has been
played. . . . Hilda Wangel is perhaps the most detestable character
in the drama's range . . . victim of nymphomania . . . deliberate
murderess . . . mean, cheap, hateful, stands out in dishonourable
distinctness."

" Ibsen has written some very vile and vulgar plays . . . *The
Master Builder* bids fair to raise a mausoleum in which the Ibsen
craze may be conveniently buried and consigned to oblivion."

Some critics (Mr. A. B. Walkley among them), who
had hitherto been favourably disposed towards Ibsen,
were baffled and annoyed by *The Master Builder.* On
the other hand, a good many people whose appreciation
of the earlier plays had been lukewarm, to say the least,
found the history of Solness and Hilda enthralling. For
example, the play found an unexpected champion in the
person of Mr. G. R. Sims, who wrote:

The strength of the story, the earnestness of the dramatic purpose,
the " actuality " of everything and everybody, amply atoned for the
occasional eccentricity of the dialogue. And it was all so "frightfully thrilling." I read *The Master Builder*, and it amused me. I
went to see *The Master Builder*, and it got hold of me and held me
as in a vice. I forgot that I was in a theatre witnessing a play.
There were no actors and actresses upon the stage. A man and
woman were living their lives in a home circle without stage trick or
device—only the fourth wall was down and I could see what was
going on.

Parodies of *The Master Builder* swarmed in the comic
journals, while the serious papers were full of more or

less serious attempts to interpret the symbolism of the play. In the *Pall Mall Gazette*, for example, I was guilty of a detailed demonstration that Solness typified Mr. Gladstone, Hilda the Irish Party, and so forth. My argument was apparently irrefutable—at least it was not refuted. In the *Westminster Gazette* during the month of March there appeared a long correspondence on the subject of Mrs. Solness's dolls, arising out of the incident narrated in the following letter:

To the Editor of " The Westminster Gazette."

"SIR,—As nothing in *The Master Builder* has exercised the minds of the critics and the public so much as Mrs. Solness's ' nine lovely dolls,' you will perhaps allow me to put on record a little incident connected with them which strikes me as curious. At a recent first-night, I happened to be seated just behind a well-known critic. He turned round to me, and said, ' I want you to tell me what is *your* theory of those " nine lovely dolls." Of course one can see that they are entirely symbolical.' ' I am not so sure of that,' I replied, remembering a Norwegian cousin of my own who treasured a favourite doll until she was nearer thirty than twenty, and may do so, for aught I know, to this day. ' They, of course, " symbolise" the unsatisfied passion of motherhood in Mrs. Solness's heart; but I have very little doubt that Ibsen makes use of this " symbol" because he has observed a similar case, or cases, in real life.' ' What!' cried the critic. ' He has seen a grown-up, a middle-aged, woman continuing to " live with " her dolls!' I was about to say that it did not seem to me so very improbable, when a lady who was seated next me, a total stranger to both of us, leant forward and said, ' Excuse my interrupting you, but it may perhaps interest you to know that *I have three dolls to which I am deeply attached!*' I will not be so rude as to conjecture this lady's age; but we may be sure that a very young woman would not have had the courage to make such an avowal. Does it not seem that Ibsen knows a thing or two about human nature—English as well as

Norwegian—which we dramatic critics, though bound by our calling to be subtle psychologists, have not yet fathomed?

" I am, Sir, your obedient servant,
"WILLIAM ARCHER.

"March 6."

In the course of the correspondence, one very apposite anecdote was quoted from an American paper, the *Argonaut:*

> "An old Virginia lady said to a friend, on finding a treasured old cup cracked by a careless maid, ' I know of nothing to compare with the affliction of losing a handsome piece of old china.' ' Surely,' said the friend, ' it is not so bad as losing one's children.' ' Yes, it is,' replied the old lady, ' for when your children die, you do have the consolations of religion, you know.'"

The first performances of *Bygmester Solness* at the leading theatres of Scandinavia did not take place for more than a fortnight after the London production. The play was acted on the same evening, March 8, 1893, at the Christiania Theatre and at the Royal Theatre, Copenhagen. In Christiania Fahlström was the original Solness, and the play was acted thirty times between 1893 and 1898. In Copenhagen, Emil Poulsen and Fru Hennings, the leading actor and actress of the theatre, created the parts of Solness and Hilda, and the play was acted twelve times in the course of 1893. In Sweden the play was produced by Lindberg (the original Oswald in *Ghosts*) at Gothenburg on March 23, 1893, and at Stockholm on April 6. It had previously been acted in the provinces by one or two local companies.

In Paris *Solness le Constructeur* was first performed by the organisation known as " L'Œuvre " at the " Bouffes

du Nord ". Theatre, April 3, 1894, Count Prozor's translation being preceded by a "conférence," by M. Camille
Mauclair. M. Lugné Poë played Solness, Mlle. Marthe
Mellot Kaia, and Hilda was played by a lady who seems
‑to have wished to remain anonymous, but who is mentioned
in the criticisms as Mlle. Wissocq. In subsequent per-
:formances (1896 and 1898) Mme. Suzanne Desprès
undertook the part of Hilda ; and it was she who played
it when "L'Œuvre" visited London (Opera Comique
Theatre) in March 1895. The same company acted
the play in Brussels (April 1894), Amsterdam (September
1894), Christiania (October 1894), Milan and Liège (May
1895). The Parisian critics seem to have agreed, for the
most part, in regarding *Solness le Constructeur* as one of
Ibsen's weaker productions. Francisque Sarcey wrote :

> Really, now, is it necessary to symbolise so much, or, as our
> Rabelais put it, to matagrabolise the brain to such an extent, in
> order to express such old and simple truths ? What annoys me is
> that when one has dissipated the dense clouds in which these great
> Scandinavian writers wrap up their idea, when one has reached the
> idea itself, it is apt to prove the most obvious and childish of truisms.
> And what annoys me still more is, that having made this discovery,
> all our young people go into ecstacies of enthusiasm. What genius !
> what profundity of thought ! It was no joke getting to the bottom
> of the symbol ; but when the task is accomplished, how rich the
> reward ! One learns this new and audacious truth, that when one
> grows old one ought to do it wisely.

M. Jules Lemaître, while showing a somewhat deeper
insight into the play, took very much the same tone.
"One does not see," he wrote, "what purpose all this
‑symbolism serves. Why should not Solness *be* what he
typifies : a writer, a man of science, a painter, a sculptor,
‑an artist of genius ? *Que nous veut cet entrepreneur de*

maçonnerie ?" At the same time, M. Lemaître reiterated his fixed idea that all that is essential in Ibsen's philosophy is to be found in George Sand. On the other hand, M. Maurice Maeterlinck contributed to the *Figaro* an essay, which he afterwards re-wrote and included in his volume, *Le Trésor des Humble*, under the title of "Le Tragique Quotidien." It was in this paper that he gave utterance to his famous paradox (I quote from Mr. Alfred Sutro's translation) :

> I have grown to believe that an old man, seated in his armchair, waiting patiently with his lamp beside him, giving unconscious ear to all the eternal laws that reign about his house, interpreting, without comprehending, the silence of doors and windows and the quivering voice of the light, submitting with bent head to the presence of his soul and his destiny, . . . I have grown to believe that he, motionless as he is, does yet live in reality a deeper, more human and more universal life than the lover who strangles his mistress, the captain who conquers in battle, or "the husband who avenges his honour."

Of the play itself M. Maeterlinck wrote :

> What is it that, in *The Master Builder*, the poet has added to life, thereby making it appear so strange, so profound, so disquieting beneath its trivial surface ? The discovery is not easy, and the old master hides from us more than one secret. It would even seem as though what he wished to say were but little by the side of what he has been compelled to say. He has freed certain powers of the soul that have never yet been free, and it may well be that these have held him in thrall. . . . Hilda and Solness are, I believe, the first characters in drama who feel, for an instant, that they are living in the atmosphere of the soul ; and the discovery of this essential life that exists in them, beyond the life of every day, comes fraught with terror.

One may doubt whether Ibsen would altogether accept

his brother poet's reading of the case ; but the whole
essay is exceedingly suggestive and memorable.

The first performance of *The Master Builder* in America
took place at the Carnegie Lyceum, New York, January 16, 1900, with the following cast :

Halvard Solness	. . .	WILLIAM H. PASCOE
Mrs. Solness	. . . .	JOSEPHINE WYNDHAM
Dr. Herdal	. . . .	JOHN STEPPLINGS
Knut Brovik	. . . .	RALPH YOERG
Ragnar Brovik .	. . .	FREDERICK G. LEWIS
Kaia Fosli	. . . .	GRACE FISHER
Hilda Wangel .	. . .	FLORENCE KAHN

This performance was repeated at the New National
Theatre, Washington, January 19, and at the Tremont
Theatre, Boston, January 23. The version used was the
work of Mr. Charles Henry Meltzer. It cannot be said
that the American critics were much more appreciative
than their English brethren. The *New York Herald*, in
an article headed " Ibsen's Wildest Play," declared that :
" The drama is so essentially a study of some very occult
idea in Ibsen's mind that it takes little or no hold upon
an audience. The plot is simply stupid and the effects
and the climax are totally without warrant. They have
no connection with anything that has been said or done
at any previous time in the world's history. . . . The
motives are not sufficient for an American theatre-goer,
who wants something besides psychology and dreams to
account for things." Mr. Henry A. Clapp, one of the
leading critics of Boston, wrote thus in the *Advertiser :*
" The dramatist's power of expression in this work, his
ingenuity in insinuation, his skill in compelling and fixing

attention upon mere psychic phenomena, are marvellous. *The Master Builder* is to all intents and purposes void of action. Through continuous dialogue, unbroken by incident, the spirit of Halvard Solness is gradually displayed." Nevertheless, Mr. Clapp heartily disliked the play, and compared it with *King Lear*, greatly to its disadvantage. "The characters," he says, "are whimsies, fantasies, figments of a dream, invented merely for the exploitation or demonstration of some spiritual truths. What these truths are who shall say? A score of answers might be given to fit the prejudice or conviction of the spectator. Even the great cords and cables are not made plain, and the lesser threads are tangled up past all possibility of unravelling." Another Boston critic (in the *Traveler*) was more emphatic. "If Ibsen," he said, "were not the author of *The Master Builder*, it would be produced nowhere unless in the harmless ward of an insane asylum. The use of idiots to point a moral and adorn a tale may be esteemed as art in Norway, but Boston intellectuality fortunately has not yet reached the proper degree of morbidness to appreciate it." One cannot help wondering whether, if *The Master Builder* could have come within the ken of Ralph Waldo Emerson, his Concord intellectuality might not have seen in it a thing or two which escaped the intellectuality of New York, Washington, and Boston itself.

WILLIAM ARCHER.

LONDON, *June* 10, 1901.

PERSONS

HALVARD SOLNESS, *the Master Builder.*

ALINE SOLNESS, *his wife.*

DOCTOR HERDAL, *physician.*

KNUT BROVIK, *formerly an architect, now in* SOLNESS'S *employment.*

RAGNAR BROVIK, *his son, draughtsman.*

KAIA FOSLI, *his niece, book-keeper.*

MISS HILDA WANGEL.

Some Ladies.

A Crowd in the street.

The action passes in and about the house of SOLNESS.

THE MASTER BUILDER

ACT FIRST

A plainly furnished work-room in the house of
HALVARD SOLNESS. *Folding doors on the left lead
out to the hall. On the right is the door leading
to the inner rooms of the house. At the back is
an open door into the draughtsmen's office. In
front, on the left, a desk with books, papers and
writing materials. Further back than the folding
door, a stove. In the right-hand corner, a sofa,
a table, and one or two chairs. On the table
a water-bottle and glass. A smaller table, with
a rocking-chair and arm-chair, in front on the
right. Lighted lamps with shades on the table
in the draughtsmen's office, on the table in the
corner, and on the desk.*

In the draughtsmen's office sit KNUT BROVIK *and his
son* RAGNAR, *occupied with plans and calculations.
At the desk in the outer office stands* KAIA FOSLI,

A

writing in the ledger. KNUT BROVIK *is a spare old man with white hair and beard. He wears a rather threadbare but well-brushed black coat, spectacles, and a somewhat discoloured white neckcloth.* RAGNAR BROVIK *is a well-dressed, light-haired man of about thirty, who stoops a little.* KAIA FOSLI *is a slightly built girl, a little over twenty, carefully dressed, and delicate-looking. She has a green shade over her eyes.—All three go on working for some time in silence.*

KNUT BROVIK.

[*Rises suddenly, as if in distress, from the table; breathes heavily and laboriously as he comes forward into the doorway.*] No, I can t bear it much longer !

KAIA.

[*Going up to him.*] You're feeling very ill this evening, aren't you, Uncle ?

BROVIK.

Oh, I seem to get worse every day.

RAGNAR.

[*Has risen and advances.*] You ought to go home, father. Try to get a little sleep——

BROVIK.

[*Impatiently.*] Go to bed, I suppose ? Would you have me stifled outright ?

KAIA.

Then take a little walk.

RAGNAR.

Yes, do. I'll come with you.

BROVIK.

[*With warmth.*] I will not go till he comes ! I'm determined to have it out this evening with—[*in a tone of suppressed bitterness*]—with him—with the chief.

KAIA.

[*Anxiously.*] Oh no, uncle,—do wait awhile before doing *that* !

RAGNAR.

Yes, better wait, father !

BROVIK.

[*Draws his breath laboriously.*] Ha—ha—! *I* haven't much time for waiting.

KAIA.

[*Listening.*] Hush ! I hear him on the stairs.
[*All three go back to their work. A short silence.*

HALVARD SOLNESS *comes in through the hall-door. He is a man of mature age, healthy and vigorous, with close-cut curly hair, dark moustache and dark thick eyebrows. He wears a greyish-green buttoned jacket with an upstanding collar and broad lappels. On his head he wears a soft grey felt hat, and he has one or two light portfolios under his arm.*

SOLNESS.

[*Near the door, points towards the draughtsmen's office, and asks in a whisper :*] Are they gone?

KAIA.

[*Softly, shaking her head.*] No.

> [*She takes the shade off her eyes.* SOLNESS *crosses the room, throws his hat on a chair, places the portfolios on the table by the sofa, and approaches the desk again.* KAIA *goes on writing without intermission, but seems nervous and uneasy.*

SOLNESS.

[*Aloud.*] What is that you're entering, Miss Fosli?

KAIA.

[*Starts.*] Oh, it's only something that——

SOLNESS.

Let me look at it, Miss Fosli. [*Bends over her, pretends to be looking into the ledger, and whispers:*] Kaia!

KAIA.

[*Softly, still writing.*] Well!

SOLNESS.

Why do you always take that shade off when I come?

KAIA.

[*As before.*] I look so ugly with it on.

SOLNESS.

[*Smiling.*] Then you don't like to look ugly, Kaia?

KAIA.

[*Half glancing up at him.*] Not for all the world Not in *your* eyes.

SOLNESS.

[*Strokes her hair gently.*] Poor, poor little Kaia——

KAIA.

[*Bending her head.*] Hush, they can hear you!

[SOLNESS *strolls across the room to the right, turns and pauses at the door of the draughts-men's office.*

SOLNESS.

Has any one been here for me ?

RAGNAR.

[*Rising.*] Yes, the young couple who want a villa built out at Lövstrand.

SOLNESS.

[*Growling.*] Oh, those two ! They must wait. I'm not quite clear about the plans yet.

RAGNAR.

[*Advancing, with some hesitation.*] They were very anxious to have the drawings at once.

SOLNESS.

[*As before.*] Yes, of course—so they all are.

BROVIK.

[*Looks up.*] They say they're longing so to get into a house of their own.

SOLNESS.

Yes, yes—we know all that ! And so they're content to take whatever's offered them. They get a—a roof over their heads—an address—but nothing to call a home. No thank you ! In that case, let

them apply to somebody else. Tell them *that*, the
next time they call.

BROVIK.

[*Pushes his glasses up on to his forehead and looks
in astonishment at him.*] To somebody else? Are
you prepared to give up the commission?

SOLNESS.

[*Impatiently.*] Yes, yes, yes, devil take it! If
that's to be the way of it——. Rather that, than build
away at random. [*Vehemently.*] Besides, I know very
little about these people as yet.

BROVIK.

The people are safe enough. Ragnar knows them.
He's a friend of the family. Perfectly safe people.

SOLNESS.

Oh, safe—safe enough! That's not at all what I
mean. Good lord—don't *you* understand me either?
[*Angrily.*] I won't have anything to do with these
strangers. They may apply to whom they please, so
far as I'm concerned.

BROVIK.

[*Rising.*] Do you really mean it?

SOLNESS.

[*Sulkily.*] Yes I do.—For once in a way.

[*He comes forward.*

[BROVIK *exchanges a glance with* RAGNAR,
who makes a warning gesture. Then
BROVIK *comes into the front room.*

BROVIK.

May I have a few words with you?

SOLNESS.

Certainly.

BROVIK.

[*To* KAIA.] Just go in there for a moment, Kaia.

KAIA.

[*Uneasily.*] Oh, but uncle——

BROVIK.

Do as I say, child. And shut the door after you.

[KAIA *goes reluctantly into the draughtsmen's
office, glances anxiously and entreatingly
at* SOLNESS, *and shuts the door.*

BROVIK.

[*Lowering his voice a little.*] I don't want the poor
children to know how ill I am.

SOLNESS.

Yes, you've been looking very poorly of late.

BROVIK.

It will soon be all over with me.   My strength is ebbing from day to day.

SOLNESS.

Won't you sit down ?

BROVIK.

Thanks—may I ?

SOLNESS.

[*Placing the arm-chair more conveniently.*] Here— take this chair.—And now ?

BROVIK.

[*Has seated himself with difficulty.*] Well, you see, it's about Ragnar.   That's what weighs most upon me.   What is to become of him ?

SOLNESS.

Of course your son will stay with me as long as ever he likes.

BROVIK.

But that's just what he doesn't like. He feels that
he can't stay any longer.

SOLNESS.

Why, I should say he was very well off here. But
if he wants a rise, I shouldn't object to——

BROVIK.

No, no! It's not *that*. [*Impatiently.*] But sooner
or later he, too, must have a chance of doing something on his own account.

SOLNESS.

[*Without looking at him.*] Do you think that Ragnar
has quite talent enough to stand alone?

BROVIK.

No, that's just the heartbreaking part of it—I've
begun to have my doubts about the boy. For you've
never said so much as—as one encouraging word
about him. And yet I can't help thinking there must
be something in him—he can't possibly be without
talent.

SOLNESS.

Well, but he has learnt nothing—nothing thoroughly, I mean. Except, of course, to draw.

BROVIK.

[*Looks at him with covert hatred, and says hoarsely.*]
You had learned little enough of the business when
you were in my employment. But that didn't prevent
you from setting to work—[*breathing with difficulty*]
—and pushing your way up, and taking the wind out
of my sails—mine, and other people's.

SOLNESS.

Yes, you see—circumstances favoured me.

BROVIK.

You're right there. Everything favoured you.
But then how can you have the heart to let me go to
my grave—without having seen what Ragnar is fit
for ? And of course I'm anxious to see them married,
too—before I go.

SOLNESS.

[*Sharply.*] Is it she who wishes it ?

BROVIK.

Not Kaia so much as Ragnar—he talks about it
every day. [*Appealingly.*] You must—you *must*
help him to get some independent work now ! I
must see something that the lad has done. Do you
hear ?

SOLNESS.

[*Peevishly.*] You can't expect me to drag commissions down from the moon for him!

BROVIK.

He has the chance of a capital commission at this very moment. A big bit of work.

SOLNESS.

[*Uneasily, startled.*] Has he?

BROVIK.

If *you* would give your consent.

SOLNESS.

. What sort of work do you mean?

BROVIK.

[*With some hesitation.*] He can have the building of that villa out at Lövstrand.

SOLNESS.

That! Why I'm going to build that myself!

BROVIK.

Oh you don't much care about doing it.

SOLNESS.

[*Flaring up.*] Don't care ! I ! Who dares to say that ?

BROVIK.

You said so yourself just now.

SOLNESS.

Oh, never mind what I *say.*—Would they give Ragnar the building of that villa ?

BROVIK.

Yes. You see, he knows the family. And then— just for the fun of the thing—he's made drawings and estimates and so forth——

SOLNESS.

Are they pleased with the drawings ? The people who've got to live in the house ?

BROVIK.

Yes. If you would only look through them and approve of them——

SOLNESS.

Then they would let Ragnar build their home for them ?

BROVIK.

They were immensely pleased with his idea.   They thought it exceedingly original, they said.

SOLNESS.

Oho!   Original!   Not the old-fashioned stuff that *I'm* in the habit of turning out.

BROVIK.

It seemed to them *different*.

SOLNESS.

[*With suppressed irritation.*] So it was to see Ragnar that they came here—whilst I was out!

BROVIK.

They came to call upon you—and at the same time to ask whether you would mind retiring——

SOLNESS.

[*Angrily.*] Retire?   I?

BROVIK.

In case you thought that Ragnar's drawings——

SOLNESS.

I?   Retire in favour of your son?

BROVIK.

Retire from the agreement, they meant.

SOLNESS.

Oh, it comes to the same thing. [*Laughs angrily.*] So that's it, is it? Halvard Solness is to see about retiring now! To make room for younger men! For the very youngest, perhaps! He's got to make room! Room! Room!

BROVIK.

Why, good heavens! there's surely room for more than one single man——

SOLNESS.

Oh, there's not so very much room to spare either. But, be that as it may—I will never retire! I will never give way to anybody! Never of my own free will. Never in this world will I do *that!*

BROVIK.

[*Rises with difficulty.*] Then I am to pass out of life without any certainty? Without a gleam of happiness? Without any faith or trust in Ragnar? Without having seen a single piece of work of his doing? Is that to be the way of it?

SOLNESS.

[*Turns half aside, and mutters.*] H'm—don't ask more just now.

BROVIK.

But answer me this one thing.　Am I to pass out of life in such utter poverty?

SOLNESS.

[*Seems to struggle with himself; finally he says, in a low but firm voice :*] You must pass out of life as best you can.

BROVIK.

Then be it so.　　　　　　　[*He goes up the room.*

SOLNESS.

[*Following him, half in desperation.*] Don't you understand that I *cannot* help it?　I am what I am, and I can't change my nature!

BROVIK.

No, no; you evidently can't.　[*Reels and supports himself against the sofa-table.*] May I have a glass of water?

SOLNESS.

By all means.   [*Fills a glass and hands it to him.*

BROVIK.

Thanks.   [*Drinks and puts the glass down again.*

SOLNESS *goes up and opens the door of the*
draughtsmen's office.

SOLNESS.

Ragnar—you must come and take your father
home.

RAGNAR *rises quickly. He and* KAIA *come into*
the work-room.

RAGNAR.

What's the matter, father ?

BROVIK.

Give me your arm. Now let us go.

RAGNAR.

All right. You'd better put your things on, too,
Kaia.

SOLNESS.

Miss Fosli must stay—just a moment. There's a
letter I want written.

B

BROVIK.

[*Looks at* SOLNESS.] Good night. Sleep well—if you can.

SOLNESS.

Good night.

> [BROVIK *and* RAGNAR *go out through the hall-door.* KAIA *goes to the desk.* SOLNESS *stands with bent head, to the right, by the arm-chair.*

KAIA.

[*Dubiously.*] Is there any letter——?

SOLNESS.

[*Curtly.*] No, of course not. [*Looks sternly at her.*] Kaia!

KAIA.

[*Anxiously, in a low voice.*] Yes!

SOLNESS.

[*Points imperatively to a spot on the floor.*] Come here! At once!

KAIA.

[*Hesitatingly.*] Yes.

SOLNESS.

[*As before.*] Nearer!

KAIA.

[*Obeying.*] What do you want with me?

SOLNESS.

[*Looks at her for a while.*] Is it you I have to thank for all this?

KAIA.

No, no, don't think that!

SOLNESS.

But confess now—you want to get married!

KAIA.

[*Softly.*] Ragnar and I have been engaged for four or five years, and so——

SOLNESS.

And so you think it's time there were an end of it. Isn't that so?

KAIA.

Ragnar and Uncle say I *must*. So I suppose I'll have to give in.

SOLNESS.

[*More gently.*] Kaia, don't you really care a little bit for Ragnar, too ?

KAIA.

I cared very much for Ragnar once—before I came here to you.

SOLNESS.

But you don't now ?   Not in the least ?

KAIA.

[*Passionately, clasping her hands and holding them out towards him.*] Oh, you know very well that there's only *one* person I care for now !   One, and one only, in all the world.   I shall never care for any one else again !

SOLNESS.

Yes, you say that.   And yet you go away from me —leave me alone here with everything on my hands.

KAIA.

But couldn't I stay with you, even if Ragnar——?

SOLNESS.

[*Repudiating the idea.*] No, no, that's quite impossible.   If Ragnar leaves me and starts work on his own account, then of course he'll need you himself.

KAIA.

[*Wringing her hands.*] Oh, I feel as if I *couldn't* be separated from you ! It's quite, quite impossible !

SOLNESS.

Then be sure you get those foolish notions out of Ragnar's mind. Marry him as much as you please— [*Alters his tone.*] I mean—don't let him throw up his good situation with me. For then I can keep *you* too, my dear Kaia.

KAIA.

Oh yes, how lovely that would be, if it could only be managed.

SOLNESS.

[*Clasps her head with his two hands and whispers.*] For I *can't* get on without you, you see. I must have you with me every single day.

KAIA.

[*In nervous exaltation.*] My God ! My God !

SOLNESS.

[*Kisses her hair.*] Kaia—Kaia !

KAIA.

[*Sinks down before him.*] Oh, how good you are to me ! How unspeakably good you are !

SOLNESS.

[*Vehemently.*] Get up! For goodness' sake get up! I think I hear some one!

> [*He helps her to rise. She staggers over to the desk.* MRS. SOLNESS *enters by the door on the right. She looks thin and wasted with grief, but shows traces of bygone beauty. Blonde ringlets. Dressed with good taste, wholly in black. Speaks somewhat slowly and in a plaintive voice.*

MRS. SOLNESS.

[*In the doorway.*] Halvard!

SOLNESS.

[*Turns.*] Oh, are you there, dear——?

MRS. SOLNESS.

[*With a glance at* KAIA.] I'm afraid I'm disturbing you.

SOLNESS.

Not in the least Miss Fosli has only a short letter to write.

MRS. SOLNESS.

Yes, so I see.

SOLNESS.

What do you want with me, Aline ?

MRS. SOLNESS.

I merely wanted to tell you that Dr. Herdal is in the drawing-room. Won't you come and see him, Halvard ?

SOLNESS.

[*Looks suspiciously at her.*] H'm—is the doctor so very anxious to talk to me ?

MRS. SOLNESS.

Well, not exactly anxious. He really came to see me ; but he would like to say how-do-you-do to you at the same time.

SOLNESS.

[*Laughs to himself.*] Yes, I daresay. Well, you must ask him to wait a little.

MRS. SOLNESS.

Then you'll come in later on ?

SOLNESS.

Perhaps I will. Later on, later on, dear. Presently.

MRS. SOLNESS.

[*Glancing again at* KAIA.] Well now, don't forget, Halvard.   [*Withdraws and closes the door behind her.*

KAIA.

[*Softly.*] Oh dear, oh dear—I'm sure Mrs. Solness thinks ill of me in some way !

SOLNESS.

Oh, not in the least.   Not more than usual at any rate.   But you'd better go now, all the same, Kaia.

KAIA.

Yes, yes, now I must go.

SOLNESS.

[*Severely.*] And mind you get that matter settled for me.   Do you hear ?

KAIA.

Oh, if it only depended on *me*——

SOLNESS.

I *will* have it settled, I say !   And to-morrow too— not a day later !

KAIA.

[*Terrified.*] If there's nothing else for it, I'm quite willing to break off the engagement.

SOLNESS.

[*Angrily.*] Break it off! Are you mad? Would you think of breaking it off?

KAIA.

[*Distracted.*] Yes, if necessary. For I *must*—I *must* stay here with you! I can't leave you! That's utterly—utterly impossible!

SOLNESS.

[*With a sudden outburst.*] But deuce take it—how about Ragnar then! It's Ragnar that I——

KAIA.

[*Looks at him with terrified eyes.*] It is chiefly on Ragnar's account, that—that you——?

SOLNESS.

[*Collecting himself.*] No, no, of course not! You don't understand me either. [*Gently and softly.*] Of course it's *you* I want to keep—you above everything, Kaia. But for that very reason you must prevent Ragnar too from throwing up his situation. There, there,—now go home.

KAIA.

Yes, yes—good night, then.

SOLNESS.

Good night. [*As she is going.*] Oh ! stop a moment !
Are Ragnar's drawings in there ?

KAIA.

I didn't see him take them with him.

SOLNESS.

Then just go in and find them for me. I might
perhaps glance over them.

KAIA.

[*Happy.*] Oh yes, please do !

SOLNESS.

For your sake, Kaia dear. Now, let me have them
at once, please.

[KAIA *hurries into the draughtsmen's office,*
searches anxiously in the table-drawer
finds a portfolio and brings it with her.

KAIA.

Here are all the drawings.

SOLNESS.

Good. Put them down there on the table.

KAIA.

[*Putting down the portfolio.*] Good night, then. [*Beseechingly.*] And think kindly of me.

SOLNESS.

Oh, that I always do. Good-night, my dear little Kaia. [*Glances to the right.*] Go, go now!

MRS. SOLNESS *and* DR. HERDAL *enter by the door on the right. He is a stoutish, elderly man, with a round, good-humoured face, clean shaven, with thin, light hair, and gold spectacles.*

MRS. SOLNESS.

[*Still in the doorway.*] Halvard, I cannot keep the doctor any longer.

SOLNESS.

Well then, come in here.

MRS. SOLNESS.

[*To* KAIA, *who is turning down the desk-lamp.*] Have you finished the letter already, Miss Fosli?

KAIA.

[*In confusion.*] The letter——?

SOLNESS.

Yes, it was quite a short one.

MRS. SOLNESS.

It must have been very short.

SOLNESS.

You may go now, Miss Fosli.   And please come in good time to-morrow morning.

KAIA.

I will be sure to.   Good-night, Mrs. Solness.
[*She goes out by the hall-door.*

MRS. SOLNESS.

She must be quite an acquisition to you, Halvard, this Miss Fosli.

SOLNESS.

Yes, indeed.   She's useful in all sorts of ways.

MRS. SOLNESS.

So it seems.

DR. HERDAL.

Is she good at book-keeping, too?

SOLNESS.

Well—of course she's had a good deal of practice during these two years. And then she's so nice and obliging in every possible way.

MRS. SOLNESS.

Yes, that must be very delightful.

SOLNESS.

It *is*. Especially when one doesn't get too much of that sort of thing.

MRS. SOLNESS.

[*In a tone of gentle remonstrance.*] Can *you* say that, Halvard ?

SOLNESS.

Oh, no, no, my dear Aline ; I beg your pardon.

MRS. SOLNESS.

There's no occasion. Well then, doctor, you'll come back later on and have a cup of tea with us ?

DR. HERDAL.

I've only a professional visit to pay, and then I'll come back.

MRS. SOLNESS.

Thank you.　[*She goes out by the door on the right.*

SOLNESS.

Are you in a hurry, doctor?

DR. HERDAL.

No, not at all.

SOLNESS.

May I have a little chat with you?

DR. HERDAL.

With the greatest of pleasure.

SOLNESS.

Then let us sit down. [*He motions the doctor to take the rocking-chair, and sits down himself in the arm-chair. Looks searchingly at him.*] Tell me, did you notice anything odd about Aline?

DR. HERDAL.

Do you mean just now when she was here?

SOLNESS.

Yes, in her manner to me. Did you notice anything?

DR. HERDAL.

[*Smiling.*] Well, I admit—one couldn't well avoid noticing that your wife—h'm——

SOLNESS.

Well ?

DR. HERDAL.

—that your wife isn't particularly fond of this Miss Fosli.

SOLNESS.

Is that all ?   I've noticed that myself.

DR. HERDAL.

And I must say it doesn't surprise me.

SOLNESS.

What doesn't ?

DR. HERDAL.

That she shouldn't exactly approve of your seeing so much of another woman, all day and every day.

SOLNESS.

No, no, I suppose you're right there—and Aline too.   But it's impossible to make any change.

DR. HERDAL.

Could you not engage a clerk ?

SOLNESS.

The first man that came to hand ? No, thanks—
that would never do for me.

DR. HERDAL.

But now, if your wife—— ? Suppose, with her
delicate health, all this tries her too much ?

SOLNESS.

Well then there's no help for it—I could almost
say. I *must* keep Kaia Fosli. No one else could fill
her place.

DR. HERDAL.

No one else ?

SOLNESS.

[*Curtly.*] No, no one.

DR. HERDAL.

[*Drawing his chair closer.*] Now listen to me, my
dear Mr. Solness. May I ask you a question, quite
between ourselves ?

SOLNESS.

By all means.

Dr. Herdal.

Women, you see—in certain matters, they have a deucedly keen intuition——

Solness.

They have indeed. There's not the least doubt of that. But——

Dr. Herdal.

Well, tell me now—if your wife can't endure this Kaia Fosli—— ?

Solness.

Well, what then ?

Dr. Herdal.

—hasn't she got just—just the least little bit of reason for this involuntary dislike ?

Solness.

[*Looks at him and rises.*] Oho !

Dr. Herdal.

Now don't be offended—but *hasn't* she ?

Solness.

[*With curt decision.*] No.

DR. HERDAL.

No reason of any sort ?

SOLNESS.

No other reason than her own suspicious nature.

DR. HERDAL.

I know you've known a good many women in your time.

SOLNESS.

Yes, I have.

DR. HERDAL.

And have been a good deal taken with some of them, too ?

SOLNESS.

Oh yes, I don't deny it.

DR. HERDAL.

But as regards Miss Fosli, then—there's nothing of that sort in the case ?

SOLNESS.

No ; nothing at all—on *my* side.

DR. HERDAL.

But on her side ?

SOLNESS.

I don't think you have any right to ask that question, doctor.

DR. HERDAL.

Well, you know, we were discussing your wife's intuition.

SOLNESS.

So we were. And for that matter—[*lowers his voice*]—Aline's intuition, as you call it—in a certain sense, it's not been so far out.

DR. HERDAL.

Aha ! there we have it !

SOLNESS.

[*Sits down.*] Doctor Herdal—I'm going to tell you a strange story—if you care to listen to it.

DR. HERDAL.

I like listening to strange stories.

SOLNESS.

Very well then. I daresay you recollect that I took Knut Brovik and his son into my service—after the old man's business had gone to the dogs.

DR. HERDAL.

Yes, so I've understood.

SOLNESS.

You see, they really are clever fellows, these two. Each of them has talent in his way. But then the son took it into his head to get engaged; and the next thing, of course, was that he wanted to get married—and begin to build on his own account. That's the way with all these young people.

DR. HERDAL.

[*Laughing.*] Yes, they've a bad habit of wanting to marry.

SOLNESS.

Just so. But of course that didn't suit *my* plans; for I needed Ragnar myself—and the old man, too. He's exceedingly good at calculating bearing-strains and cubic contents—and all that sort of devilry, you know.

DR. HERDAL.

Oh yes, no doubt that's very important.

SOLNESS.

Yes, it is. But Ragnar was absolutely bent on setting to work for himself. He wouldn't hear of anything else.

DR. HERDAL.

But he has stayed with you all the same.

SOLNESS.

Yes, I'll tell you how that came about. One day this girl, Kaia Fosli, came to see them on some errand or other. She had never been here before. And when I saw how utterly infatuated they were with each other, the thought occurred to me: if only I could get her into the office here, then perhaps Ragnar too would stay where he is.

DR. HERDAL.

That was not at all a bad idea.

SOLNESS.

Yes, but at the time I didn't breathe a word of what was in my mind. I merely stood and looked at her, and kept wishing intently that I could have her here. Then I talked to her a little, in a friendly way—about one thing and another. And then she went away

DR. HERDAL.

Well?

SOLNESS.

Well then, next day, pretty late in the evening, when old Brovik and Ragnar had gone home, she came here again, and behaved as if I had made an arrangement with her.

DR. HERDAL.

An arrangement? What about?

SOLNESS.

About the very thing my mind had been fixed on. But I hadn't said one single word about it.

DR. HERDAL.

That was most extraordinary.

SOLNESS.

Yes, wasn't it? And now she wanted to know what she was to do here, whether she could begin the very next morning, and so forth.

DR. HERDAL.

Don't you think she did it in order to be with her sweetheart?

SOLNESS.

That was what occurred to me at first. But no, that wasn't it. She seemed to drift quite away from *him*—when once she had come here to me.

DR. HERDAL.

She drifted over to you, then ?

SOLNESS.

Yes, entirely. If I happen to look at her when her back is turned, I can tell that she feels it. She quivers and trembles the moment I come near her. What do you think of that ?

DR. HERDAL.

H'm—that's not very hard to explain.

SOLNESS.

Well, but what about the other thing ? That she believed I had said to her what I had only wished and willed—silently—inwardly—to myself ? What do you say to that ? Can you explain that, Dr. Herdal ?

DR. HERDAL.

No, I won't undertake to do that.

SOLNESS.

I felt sure you wouldn't; and so I've never cared to talk about it till now. But it's a cursed nuisance to me in the long run, you understand. Here have I got to go on day after day pretending——. And it's a shame to treat her so, too, poor girl. [*Vehemently.*] But I *can't* do anything else. For if *she* runs away from me—then Ragnar will be off too.

DR. HERDAL.

And you haven't told your wife the rights of the story?

SOLNESS.

No.

DR. HERDAL.

Then why on earth don't you?

SOLNESS.

[*Looks fixedly at him and says in a low voice:*] Because I seem to find a sort of—of salutary self-torture in allowing Aline to do me an injustice.

DR. HERDAL.

[*Shakes his head.*] I don't in the least understand what you mean.

SOLNESS.

Well, you see, it's like paying off a little bit of a huge, immeasurable debt——

DR. HERDAL.

To your wife ?

SOLNESS.

Yes; and that always helps to relieve one's mind a little. One can breathe more freely for a while, you see.

DR. HERDAL.

No, goodness knows, I don't see at all——

SOLNESS.

[*Breaking off, rises again.*] Well, well, well—then we won't talk any more about it. [*He saunters across the room, returns, and stops beside the table. Looks at the doctor with a sly smile.*] I suppose you think you've drawn me out nicely now, doctor ?

DR. HERDAL.

[*With some irritation.*] Drawn you out ? Again I haven't the faintest notion what you mean, Mr. Solness.

SOLNESS.

Oh come, out with it ; for I've seen it quite clearly, you know.

DR. HERDAL.

What have you seen ?

SOLNESS.

[*In a low voice, slowly.*] That you've been quietly keeping an eye upon me.

DR. HERDAL.

That *I* have !   And why in all the world should I do *that ?*

SOLNESS.

Because you think that I——[*Passionately.*] Well, devil take it—you think the same of me as Aline does.

DR. HERDAL.

And what does *she* think about you ?

SOLNESS.

[*Having recovered his self-control.*] She has begun to think that I'm—that I'm—ill.

DR. HERDAL.

Ill !   *You !*   She has never hinted such a thing to me.   Why, what can she think is the matter with you ?

SOLNESS.

[*Leans over the back of the chair and whispers.*]
Aline has made up her mind that I am mad. *That's*
what she thinks.

DR. HERDAL.

[*Rising.*] Why, my dear, good fellow——!

SOLNESS.

Yes, on my soul she does ! I tell you it's so ! And
she has got you to think the same. Oh, I can
assure you, doctor, I see it in your face as clearly as
possible. You don't take me in so easily, I can tell
you.

DR. HERDAL.

[*Looks at him in amazement.*] Never, Mr. Solness
—never has such a thought entered my mind.

SOLNESS.

[*With an incredulous smile.*] Really ? Has it not ?

DR. HERDAL.

No, never ! Nor your wife's mind either, I'm con-
vinced. I could almost swear to that.

SOLNESS.

Well, I wouldn't advise you to. For, in a certain sense, you see, perhaps—perhaps she's not so far wrong in thinking something of the kind.

DR. HERDAL.

Come now, I really must say——

SOLNESS.

[*Interrupting with a sweep of his hand.*] Well, well, my dear doctor—don't let us discuss this any further. We had better agree to differ. [*Changes to a tone of quiet merriment.*] But look here now, doctor—h'm——

DR. HERDAL.

Well?

SOLNESS.

Since you don't believe that I am—ill—and crazy —and mad, and so forth——

DR. HERDAL.

What then?

SOLNESS.

Then I daresay you fancy that I'm an extremely happy man? ·

DR. HERDAL.

Is *that* mere fancy ?

SOLNESS.

[*Laughs.*] No, no—of course not ! Heaven forbid !
Only think—to be Solness the master builder ! Halvard Solness ! What could be more delightful ?

DR. HERDAL.

Yes, I must say it seems to me you've had the luck
on your side to an astounding degree.

SOLNESS.

[*Suppresses a gloomy smile.*] So I have. I can't
complain on *that* score.

DR. HERDAL.

First of all that grim old robbers'-castle was burnt
down for you. And that was certainly a great piece
of luck.

SOLNESS.

[*Seriously.*] It was the home of Aline's family.
Remember that.

DR. HERDAL.

Yes, it must have been a great grief to *her*. :

SOLNESS.

She hasn't got over it to this day—not in all these twelve or thirteen years.

DR. HERDAL.

Ah, but what followed must have been the worst blow for her.

SOLNESS.

The one thing with the other.

DR. HERDAL.

But you—yourself—*you* rose upon the ruins. You began as a poor boy from a country village—and now you're at the head of your profession. Ah, yes, Mr. Solness, you've undoubtedly had the luck on your side.

SOLNESS.

[*Looks doubtfully across at him.*] Yes, but that's just what makes me so horribly afraid.

DR. HERDAL.

Afraid? Because you have the luck on your side!

SOLNESS.

It terrifies me—terrifies me every hour of the day. For sooner or later the luck must turn, you see.

DR. HERDAL.

Oh nonsense! What should make the luck turn?

SOLNESS.

[*With firm assurance.*] The younger generation.

DR. HERDAL.

Pooh! The younger generation! You're not laid on the shelf yet, I should hope. Oh no—your position here is probably firmer now than it has ever been.

SOLNESS.

The luck *will* turn. I know it—I feel the day approaching. Some one or other will take it into his head to say: Give *me* a chance! And then all the rest will come clamouring after him, and shake their fists at me and shout: Make room—make room—make room! Yes, just you see, doctor—presently the younger generation will come knocking at my door——

DR. HERDAL.

[*Laughing.*] Well, and what if they do?

SOLNESS.

What if they do? Then there's an end of Halvard Solness. [*There is a knock at the door on the left. Starts.*] What's that? Didn't you hear something?

DR. HERDAL.

Some one is knocking at the door.

SOLNESS.

[*Loudly.*] Come in.

HILDA WANGEL *enters through the hall door. She is of middle height, supple, and delicately built. Somewhat sunburnt. Dressed in a tourist costume, with skirt caught up for walking, a sailor's collar open at the throat, and a small sailor hat on her head. Knapsack on back, plaid shawl in strap, and alpenstock.*

HILDA.

[*Goes straight up to* SOLNESS, *her eyes sparkling with happiness.*] Good evening!

SOLNESS.

[*Looks doubtfully at her.*] Good evening——

HILDA.

[*Laughs.*] I almost believe you don't recognise me!

SOLNESS.

No—I must admit that—just for the moment——

DR. HERDAL.

[*Approaching.*] But *I* recognise you, my dear young lady——

HILDA.

[*Pleased.*] Oh, is it you that——

DR. HERDAL.

Of course it is. [*To* SOLNESS.] We met at one of the mountain stations this summer. [*To* HILDA.] What became of the other ladies?

HILDA.

Oh, they went westward.

DR. HERDAL.

They didn't much like all the fun we used to have in the evenings.

HILDA.

No, I believe they didn't.

D

DR. HERDAL.

[*Holds up his finger at her.*] And I'm afraid it can't be denied that you flirted a little with us.

HILDA.

Well, that was better fun than to sit there knitting stockings with all those old women.

DR. HERDAL.

[*Laughs.*] There I entirely agree with you!

SOLNESS.

Have you come to town this evening?

HILDA.

Yes, I've just arrived.

DR. HERDAL.

Quite alone, Miss Wangel?

HILDA.

Oh yes!

SOLNESS.

Wangel? Is your name Wangel?

HILDA.

[*Looks in amused surprise at him.*] Yes, of course it is.

SOLNESS.

Then you must be the daughter of the district doctor up at Lysanger?

HILDA.

[*As before.*] Yes, who else's daughter should I be?

SOLNESS.

Oh, then I suppose we met up there, that summer when I was building a tower on the old church.

HILDA.

[*More seriously.*] Yes, of course it was then we met.

SOLNESS.

Well, that's a long time ago.

HILDA.

[*Looks hard at him.*] It's just the ten years.

SOLNESS.

You must have been a mere child then, I should think.

HILDA.

[*Carelessly.*] Well, I was twelve or thirteen.

DR. HERDAL.

Is this the first time you've ever been up to town, Miss Wangel?

HILDA.

Yes, it is indeed.

SOLNESS.

And don't you know any one here ?

HILDA.

Nobody but you.   And of course, your wife.

SOLNESS.

So you know *her*, too ?

HILDA.   .

Only a little.   We spent a few days together at the
sanatorium.

SOLNESS.

Ah, up there ?

HILDA.

She said I might come and pay her a visit if ever
I came up to town. [*Smiles.*] Not that that was
necessary.

SOLNESS.

Odd that she should never have mentioned it.

> [HILDA *puts her stick down by the stove, takes
> off the knapsack and lays it and the plaid
> on the sofa.* DR. HERDAL *offers to help her.*
> SOLNESS *stands and gazes at her.*

HILDA.

[*Going towards him.*] Well, now I must ask you to let me spend the night here.

SOLNESS.

I'm sure we can manage that.

HILDA.

For I've no other clothes than those I stand in, except a change of linen in my knapsack. And that has to go to the wash, for it's very dirty.

SOLNESS.

Oh yes, we'll see to that. Now I'll just let my wife know——

DR. HERDAL.

Meanwhile I'll visit my patient.

SOLNESS.

Yes, do ; and come again later on.

DR. HERDAL.

[*Playfully, with a glance at* HILDA.] Oh that I will, you may be very certain ! [*Laughs.*] So your prediction has come true, Mr. Solness !

SOLNESS

How so?

Dr. Herdal.

The younger generation *did* come knocking at your door.

Solness.

[*Cheerfully.*] Yes, but in a very different way from what I meant.

Dr. Herdal.

Very different, yes. That's undeniable.

> [*He goes out by the hall-door.* Solness *opens the door on the right and speaks into the side room.*

Solness.

Aline! Will you come in here, please. Here's a friend of yours—Miss Wangel.

Mrs. Solness.

[*Appears in the doorway.*] Who do you say it is? [*Sees* Hilda.] Oh, is it you, Miss Wangel? [*Goes up to her and offers her hand.*] So you've come to town after all.

Solness.

Miss Wangel has this moment arrived; and she would like to stay the night here.

Mrs. Solness.

Here with us? Oh yes, with pleasure.

SOLNESS.

So as to get her things a little in order, you see.

MRS. SOLNESS.

I will do the best I can for you. It's no more than my duty. I suppose your trunk is coming on later?

HILDA.

I *have* no trunk.

MRS. SOLNESS.

Well, it will be all right, I daresay. In the meantime, you must excuse my leaving you here with my husband until I can get a room made a little comfortable for you.

SOLNESS.

. Can't we give her one of the nurseries? *They* are all ready as it is.

MRS. SOLNESS.

Oh yes. There we have room and to spare. [*To* HILDA.] Sit down now and rest a little.

> [*She goes out to the right.* HILDA, *with her hands behind her back, strolls about the room and looks at various objects.* SOLNESS *stands in front, beside the table, also with his hands behind his back, and follows her with his eyes.*

HILDA.

[*Stops and looks at him.*] Have you several nurseries ?

SOLNESS.

There are three nurseries in the house.

HILDA.

That's a lot. Then I suppose you have a great many children ?

SOLNESS.

No. We have no child. But now *you* can be the child here, for the time being.

HILDA.

For to-night, yes. I sha'n't cry. I mean to sleep as sound as a stone.

SOLNESS.

Yes, you must be very tired, I should think.

HILDA.

Oh no! But all the same—— It's so delicious to lie and dream.

SOLNESS.

Do you dream much of nights ?

HILDA.

Oh yes ! Almost always.

SOLNESS.

What do you dream about most ?

HILDA.

I sha'n't tell you to-night. Another time—perhaps.

> [*She again strolls about the room, stops at the
> desk and turns over the books and papers
> a little.*

SOLNESS.

[*Approaching.*] Are you searching for anything ?

HILDA.

No, I'm merely looking at all these things. [*Turns.*]
Perhaps I mustn't ?

SOLNESS.

Oh, by all means.

HILDA.

Is it you that write in this great ledger ?

SOLNESS.

No, it's my book-keeper.

HILDA.

Is it a woman ?

SOLNESS.

[*Smiles.*] Yes.

HILDA.

One you employ here, in your office ?

SOLNESS.

Yes.

HILDA.

Is she married ?

SOLNESS.

No, she's single.

HILDA.

Ah !

SOLNESS.

But I believe she's soon going to be married.

HILDA.

That's a good thing for *her*.

SOLNESS.

But not such a good thing for *me*. For then I shall have nobody to help me.

HILDA.

Can't you get hold of some one else who'll do just as well ?

SOLNESS.

Perhaps *you* would stop here and—and write in the ledger ?

HILDA.

[*Measures him with a glance.*] Yes, I daresay!
No, thanks—nothing of that sort for *me*—[*She again
strolls across the room, and sits down in the rocking-
chair.* SOLNESS *too goes to the table.* HILDA *continues :*]—for there must surely be other things than
that to be done here. [*Looks smilingly at him.*] Don't
you think so, too ?

SOLNESS.

Of course. First and foremost, I suppose you want
to make a round of the shops, and get yourself up
in the height of fashion.

HILDA.

[*Amused.*] No, I think I shall let *that* alone.

SOLNESS.

Indeed !

HILDA.

For you must know I've run through all my
money.

SOLNESS.

[*Laughs.*] Neither trunk nor money, then !

HILDA

Neither one nor the other. But never mind—it
doesn't matter now.

SOLNESS.

Come now, I like you for *that*.

HILDA.

Only for *that?*

SOLNESS.

For that among other things. [*Sits in the arm-chair.*] Is your father alive still?

HILDA.

Yes, father's alive.

SOLNESS.

Perhaps you're thinking of studying here?

HILDA.

No, that hadn't occurred to me.

SOLNESS.

But I suppose you'll be stopping for some time?

HILDA.

That must depend upon circumstances. [*She sits awhile rocking herself and looking at him, half seriously, half with a suppressed smile. Then she takes off her hat and puts it on the table in front of her.*] Mr. Solness!

SOLNESS.

Well?

HILDA.

Have you a very bad memory?

SOLNESS.

A bad memory? No, not that I'm aware of.

HILDA.

Then haven't you anything to say to me about what happened up there?

SOLNESS.

[*In momentary surprise.*] Up at Lysanger? [*Indifferently.*] Why, it was nothing much to talk about, it seems to me.

HILDA.

[*Looks reproachfully at him.*] How can you sit there and say such things?

SOLNESS.

Well, then, *you* talk to *me* about it.

HILDA.

When the tower was finished, we had grand doings in the town.

SOLNESS.

Yes, I sha'n't easily forget that day.

HILDA.

[*Smiles.*] Won't you?   That's good of you !

SOLNESS.

Good ?

HILDA.

There was music in the churchyard—and many, many hundreds of people. We school-girls were dressed in white ; and we all carried flags.

SOLNESS.

Ah yes, those flags—I can tell you I remember them !

HILDA.

Then you climbed up over the scaffolding, straight to the very top ; and you had a great wreath with you ; and you hung that wreath right away up on the weathercock.

SOLNESS.

[*Curtly interrupting.*] I always did that in those days.   It's an old custom.

HILDA.

It was so wonderfully thrilling to stand below and

look up at you, Fancy, if he should fall over ! He—
the master builder himself !

SOLNESS.

[*As if to lead her away from the subject.*] Yes, yes,
yes, that might very well have happened, too. For
one of those white-frocked little devils,—she went on
in such a way, and screamed up at me so——

HILDA.

[*Sparkling with pleasure.*] '' Hurra for Mr. Solness !''
Yes !

SOLNESS.

—and waved and flourished with her flag so that
I—so that it almost made me giddy to look at it.

HILDA.

[*In a lower voice, seriously.*] That little devil—
that was *I.*

SOLNESS.

[*Fixes his eyes steadily upon her.*] I'm sure of that
now. It *must* have been you.

HILDA.

[*Lively again.*] Oh, it was so gloriously thrilling !
I couldn't have believed there was a builder in the
whole world that could have built such a tremendously

high tower. And then, that you yourself should stand at the very top of it, as large as life! And that you shouldn't be the least bit dizzy! It was that above everything that made one—made one dizzy to think of.

SOLNESS.

How could you be so certain that I was wasn't——?

HILDA.

[*Scouting the idea.*] No indeed! Oh no! 1 knew that instinctively. For if you had been, you could never have stood up there and sung.

SOLNESS.

[*Looks at her in astonishment.*] Sung? Did I sing?

HILDA.

Yes, I should think you did.

SOLNESS.

[*Shakes his head.*] I've never sung a note in my life.

HILDA.

Yes, you sang then. It sounded like harps in the air.

SOLNESS.

[*Thoughtfully.*] This is very strange—all this.

HILDA.

[*Is silent awhile, looks at him and says in a low voice:*] But then,—it was after that—that the *real* thing happened.

SOLNESS.

The real thing?

HILDA.

[*Sparkling with vivacity.*] Yes, I surely don't need to remind you of *that*?

SOLNESS.

Oh yes, do remind me a little of *that*, too.

HILDA.

Don't you remember that a great dinner was given in your honour at the Club?

SOLNESS.

Yes, to be sure. It must have been the same after noon, for I left the place next morning.

HILDA.

And from the Club you were invited to come round to our house to supper.

E

SOLNESS.

Quite right, Miss Wangel. It's wonderful how all these trifles have impressed themselves on your mind.

HILDA.

Trifles! I like that! Perhaps it was a trifle, too, that I was *alone* in the room when you came in?

SOLNESS.

Were you alone?

HILDA.

[*Without answering him.*] You didn't call me a little devil *then*.

SOLNESS.

No, I probably didn't.

HILDA.

You said I was lovely in my white dress, and that I looked like a little princess.

SOLNESS.

I've no doubt you did, Miss Wangel.—And besides —I was feeling so buoyant and free that day——

HILDA.

And then you said that when I grew up I should be *your* princess.

SOLNESS.

[*Laughing a little.*] Dear, dear—did I say *that* too ?

HILDA.

Yes, you did. And when I asked how long I should have to wait, you said that you would come again in ten years—like a troll—and carry me off—to Spain or some such place. And you promised you would buy me a kingdom there.

SOLNESS.

[*As before.*] Yes, after a good dinner one doesn't haggle about the halfpence. But did I really *say* all that ?

HILDA.

[*Laughs to herself.*] Yes. And you told me, too, what the kingdom was to be called

SOLNESS.

Well, what was it ?

HILDA.

It was to be called the kingdom of Orangia,* you said.

---

* In the original "Appelsinia," " appelsin" meaning " orange."

SOLNESS.

Well, that was an appetizing name.

HILDA.

No, I didn't like it a bit; for it seemed as though you wanted to make game of me.

SOLNESS.

I'm sure *that* can't have been my intention.

HILDA.

No, I should hope not—considering what you did next——

SOLNESS.

What in the world did I do next?

HILDA.

Well, that's the finishing touch, if you've forgotten *that* too. I should have thought one couldn't help remembering such a thing as that.

SOLNESS.

Yes, yes, just give me a hint, and then perhaps—— Well?

HILDA.

[*Looks fixedly at him.*] You came and kissed me, Mr. Solness.

SOLNESS.

[*Open-mouthed, rising from his chair.*] *I* did!

HILDA.

Yes, indeed you did.   You took me in both your
arms, and bent my head back, and kissed me—many
times.

SOLNESS.

Now, really, my dear Miss Wangel——!

HILDA.

[*Rises.*] You surely don't mean to deny it?

SOLNESS.

Yes, I do.   I deny it altogether!

HILDA.

[*Looks scornfully at him.*] Oh, indeed

> [*She turns and goes slowly close up to the stove,
> where she remains standing motionless, her
> face averted from him, her hands behind
> her back.   Short pause.*

SOLNESS.

[*Goes cautiously up behind her.*] Miss Wangel—— !

HILDA.

[*Is silent and does not move.*]

SOLNESS.

Don't stand there like a statue. You must have dreamt all this. [*Lays his hand on her arm.*] Now just listen——

HILDA.

[*Makes an impatient movement with her arm.*]

SOLNESS.

[*As a thought flashes upon him.*] Or——! Wait a moment! There is something under all this, you may depend!

HILDA.

[*Does not move.*]

SOLNESS.

[*In a low voice, but with emphasis.*] I must have *thought* all that. I must have *wished* it—have *willed* it—have *longed* to do it. And then——. May not that be the explanation?

HILDA.

[*Is still silent.*]

SOLNESS.

[*Impatiently.*] Oh very well, deuce take it all—then I *did* do it, I suppose!

HILDA.

[*Turns her head a little, but without looking at him.*]
Then you admit it now?

SOLNESS.

Yes—whatever you like.

HILDA.

You came and put your arms round me?

SOLNESS.

Oh yes.

HILDA.

And bent my head back?

SOLNESS.

Very far back.

HILDA.

And kissed me?

SOLNESS.

Yes, I did.

HILDA.

Many times?

SOLNESS.

As many as ever you like.

HILDA.

[*Turns quickly towards him and has once more the sparkling expression of gladness in her eyes.*] Well, you see, I got it out of you at last!

SOLNESS.

[*With a slight smile.*] Yes—just think of my forgetting such a thing as that.

HILDA.

[*Again a little sulky, retreats from him.*] Oh, you've kissed so many people in your time, I suppose.

SOLNESS.

No, you mustn't think *that* of me. [HILDA *seats herself in the arm-chair.* SOLNESS *stands and leans against the rocking-chair. Looks observantly at her.*] Miss Wangel!

HILDA.

Yes!

SOLNESS.

How *was* it now? What came of all this—between us two?

HILDA.

Why, nothing more came of it. You know that quite well. For then the other guests came in, and then—bah !

SOLNESS.

Quite so ! The others came in. To think of my forgetting *that* too !

HILDA.

Oh, you haven't really forgotten anything : you're only a little ashamed of it all. I'm sure one doesn't forget things of that kind.

SOLNESS.

No, one would suppose not.

HILDA.

[*Lively again, looks at him.*] Perhaps you've even forgotten what day it was ?

SOLNESS.

What day ?

HILDA.

Yes, on what day did you hang the wreath on the tower ? Well ? Tell me at once !

SOLNESS.

H'm—I confess I've forgotten the particular day. I only know it was ten years ago. Some time in the autumn.

HILDA.

[*Nods her head slowly several times.*] It was ten years ago—on the 19th of September.

SOLNESS.

Yes, it must have been about that time. Fancy your remembering that too! [*Stops.*] But wait a moment—! Yes—it's the 19th of September to-day.

HILDA.

Yes, it is; and the ten years are gone. And you didn't come—as you had promised me.

SOLNESS.

Promised you? Threatened, I suppose you mean?

HILDA.

I don't think there was any sort of threat in *that*.

SOLNESS.

Well then, a little bit of a hoax.

HILDA.

Was that all you wanted to do ?   To hoax me ?

SOLNESS.

Well, or to have a little joke with you !   Upon my soul I don't recollect.   But it must have been something of that kind ; for you were a mere child then.

HILDA.

Oh, perhaps I wasn't quite such a child either. Not such a mere chit as you imagine.

SOLNESS.

[*Looks searchingly at her.*] Did you really and seriously expect me to come again ?

HILDA.

[*Conceals a half-teasing smile.*] Yes, indeed !   I did expect *that* of you.

SOLNESS.

That I should come back to your home, and take you away with me ?

HILDA.

Just like a troll—yes.

SOLNESS.

And make a princess of you?

HILDA.

That's what you promised.

SOLNESS.

And give you a kingdom as well?

HILDA.

[*Looks up at the ceiling.*] Why not? Of course it needn't have been an actual, every-day sort of a kingdom.

SOLNESS.

But something else just as good?.

HILDA.

Yes, at least as good. [*Looks at him a moment.*] I thought if you could build the highest church-towers in the world, you could surely manage to raise a kingdom of one sort or another as well.

SOLNESS.

[*Shakes his head.*] I can't quite make you out, Miss Wangel.

HILDA.

Can't you? To me it seems all so simple.

SOLNESS.

No, I can't make up my mind whether you mean all you say, or are simply having a joke with me.

HILDA.

[*Smiles.*] Hoaxing you, perhaps? I, too?

SOLNESS.

Yes, exactly. Hoaxing—both of us. [*Looks at her.*] Is it long since you found out that I was married?

HILDA.

I've known it all along. Why do you ask me *that?*

SOLNESS.

[*Lightly.*] Oh, well, it just occurred to me. [*Looks earnestly at her, and says in a low voice.*] What have you come for?

HILDA.

I want my kingdom. The time is up.

SOLNESS.

[*Laughs involuntarily.*] What a girl you are!

HILDA.

[*Gaily.*] Out with my kingdom, Mr. Solness! [*Raps with her fingers.*] The kingdom on the table!

SOLNESS.

[*Pushing the rocking-chair nearer and sitting down.*] Now, seriously speaking—what have you come for? What do you really want to do here?

HILDA.

Oh, first of all, I want to go round and look at all the things that you've built.

SOLNESS.

That will give you plenty of exercise.

HILDA.

Yes, I know you've built a tremendous lot.

SOLNESS.

I have indeed—especially of late years.

HILDA.

Many church-towers among the rest?   Immensely high ones?

SOLNESS.

No. I build no more church-towers now. Nor churches either.

HILDA.

What *do* you build then?

SOLNESS.

Homes for human beings.

HILDA.

[*Reflectively.*] Couldn't you build a little—a little bit of a church-tower over these homes as well?

SOLNESS.

[*Starting.*] What do you mean by *that?*

HILDA.

I mean—something that points—points up into the free air. With the vane at a dizzy height.

SOLNESS.

[*Pondering a little.*] Strange that you should say *that*—for that's just what I'm most anxious to do.

HILDA.

[*Impatiently.*] Then why don't you do it?

SOLNESS.

[*Shakes his head.*] No, the people won't have it.

HILDA.

Fancy their not wanting it!

SOLNESS.

[*More lightly.*] But now I'm building a new home for myself—just opposite here.

HILDA.

For yourself?

SOLNESS.

Yes. It's almost finished. And on that there's a tower.

HILDA.

A high tower?

SOLNESS.

Yes.

HILDA.

Very high?

SOLNESS.

No doubt people will say that it's too high—too high for a dwelling-house.

HILDA.

I'll go out and look at that tower the first thing to-morrow morning.

SOLNESS.

[*Sits with his hand under his cheek and gazes at her.*]
Tell me, Miss Wangel—what is your name? Your
Christian name, I mean?

HILDA.

Why, Hilda, of course.

SOLNESS.

[*As before.*] Hilda! Ah!

HILDA.

Don't you remember *that*? You called me Hilda
yourself—that day when you misbehaved.

SOLNESS.

Did I really?

HILDA.

But then you said "*little* Hilda"; and I didn't
like that.

SOLNESS.

Oh, you didn't like that, Miss Hilda?

HILDA.

No, not at such a time as that. But—"Princess
Hilda"—that will sound very well, I think.

F

SOLNESS.

Very well indeed.   Princess Hilda of—of—what
was to be the name of the kingdom ?

HILDA.

Pooh! I won't have anything to do with *that*
stupid kingdom.   I've set my heart upon quite a
different one !

SOLNESS.

[*Has leaned back in the chair, still gazing at her.*]
Isn't it strange—— ?   The more I think of it now, the
more it seems to me as though I had gone about all
these years torturing myself with—h'm——

HILDA.

With what ?

SOLNESS.

With the effort to recover something—some
experience, which I seemed to have forgotten.   But
I never had the least inkling of what it would be.

HILDA.

You should have tied a knot in your pocket-hand-
kerchief, Mr. Solness.

SOLNESS.

In that case, I should simply have had to go racking
my brains to discover what the knot could mean.

HILDA.

Oh yes, I suppose there are trolls of *that* kind in the world, too.

SOLNESS.

[*Rises slowly.*] What a good thing it is that *you* have come to me now.

HILDA.

[*Looks deeply into his eyes.*] *Is* it a good thing?

SOLNESS.

For I've been so lonely here. I've been gazing so helplessly at it all. [*In a lower voice.*] I must tell you—I've begun to be so afraid—so terribly afraid of the younger generation.

HILDA.

[*With a little snort of contempt.*] Pooh—is the younger generation a thing to be afraid of?

SOLNESS.

It is indeed. And that's why I've locked and barred myself in. [*Mysteriously.*] I tell you the younger generation will one day come and thunder at my door! They'll break in upon me!

HILDA.

Then I should say you ought to go out and open the door to the younger generation.

SOLNESS.

Open the door?

HILDA.

Yes. Let them come in to you on friendly terms, as it were.

SOLNESS.

No, no, no! The younger generation—it means retribution, you see. It comes, as if under a new banner, heralding the turn of fortune.

HILDA.

[*Rises, looks at him, and says with a quivering twitch of her lips.*] Can *I* be of any use to you, Mr. Solness?

SOLNESS.

Yes, you can indeed ! For you, too, come—under a new banner, it seems to me. Youth marshalled against youth—— !

DR. HERDAL *comes in by the hall-door.*

DR. HERDAL.

What—you and Miss Wangel here still?

SOLNESS.

Yes. We've had no end of things to talk about.

HILDA.

Both old and new.

DR. HERDAL.

Have you reǎlly ?

HILDA.

Oh, it has been the greatest fun. For Mr. Solness —he has such a miraculous memory. All the least little details he remembers instantly.

MRS. SOLNESS *enters by the door on the right.*

MRS. SOLNESS.

Well, Miss Wangel, your room is quite ready for you now.

HILDA.

Oh, how kind you are to me !

SOLNESS,

[*To* MRS. SOLNESS.] The nursery ?

MRS. SOLNESS.

Yes, the middle one. But first let us go in to supper.

SOLNESS.

[*Nods to* HILDA.] Hilda shall sleep in the nursery.

MRS. SOLNESS.

[*Looks at him.*] Hilda?

SOLNESS.

Yes, Miss Wangel's name is Hilda.   I knew her
when she was a child.

MRS. SOLNESS.

Did you really, Halvard?   Well, shall we go?
Supper is on the table.

> [*She takes* DR. HERDAL'S *arm and goes out
> with him to the right.* HILDA *has mean-
> while been collecting her travelling things.*

HILDA.

[*Softly and rapidly to* SOLNESS.] Is it true, what
you said?   *Can* I be of use to you?

SOLNESS.

[*Takes the things from her.*] *You* are the very one
I have most needed.

HILDA.

[*Looks at him with happy, wondering eyes and clasps
her hands.*] Oh heavens, how lovely——!

SOLNESS.

[*Eagerly*]. What—— ?

HILDA.

Then I *have* my kingdom !

SOLNESS.

[*Involuntarily.*] Hilda—— !

HILDA.

[*Again with the quivering twitch of her lips.*] *Almost*—I was going to say.

[*She goes out to the right,* SOLNESS *follows her.*

ACT SECOND

*A prettily furnished small drawing-room in the house
of* SOLNESS. *In the back, a glass-door leading out
to the verandah and garden. The right-hand
corner is cut off transversely by a large bay-window,
in which are flower-stands. The left-hand corner
is similarly cut off by a transverse wall, in which is
a small door papered like the wall. On each side,
an ordinary door. In front, on the right, a console
table with a large mirror over it. Well-filled stands
of plants and flowers. In front, on the left, a sofa
with a table and chairs. Further back, a bookcase. Well forward in the room, before the bay
window, a small table and some chairs. It is
early in the day.*

SOLNESS *sits by the little table with* RAGNAR BROVIK'S
*portfolio open in front of him. He is turning
the drawings over and closely examining some of
them.* MRS. SOLNESS *walks about noiselessly
with a small watering-pot attending to her*

flowers. She is dressed in black as before. Her hat, cloak and parasol lie on a chair near the mirror. Unobserved by her, SOLNESS *now and again follows her with his eyes. Neither of them speaks.*

KAIA FOSLI *enters quietly by the door on the left.*

SOLNESS.

[*Turns his head, and says in an off-hand tone of indifference.*] Well, is that you?

KAIA.

I merely wished to let you know I've come.

SOLNESS.

Yes, yes, that's all right. Hasn't Ragnar come too?

KAIA.

No, not yet. He had to wait a little while to see the doctor. But he's coming presently to hear——

SOLNESS.

How is the old man to-day?

KAIA.

Not well. He begs you to excuse him, for he must keep his bed to-day.

SOLNESS.

Quite so; by all means let him rest. But now, get to your work.

KAIA.

Yes. [*Pauses at the door.*] Do you wish to speak to Ragnar when he comes?

SOLNESS.

No—I don't know that I've anything special to say to him.

> [KAIA *goes out again to the left.* SOLNESS *remains seated, turning over the drawings.*

MRS. SOLNESS.

[*Over beside the plants.*] I wonder if *he* isn't going to die now, as well?

SOLNESS.

[*Looks up at her.*] As well as who?

MRS. SOLNESS.

[*Without answering.*] Yes, yes—depend upon it, Halvard, old Brovik's going to die too. You'll see that he will.

SOLNESS.

My dear Aline, oughtn't you to go out for a little walk?

MRS. SOLNESS.

Yes, I suppose I ought to.

> [*She continues to attend to the flowers.*

SOLNESS.

[*Bending over the drawings.*] Is she still asleep ?

MRS. SOLNESS.

[*Looking at him.*] Is it Miss Wangel you're sitting there thinking about ?

SOLNESS.

[*Indifferently.*] I just happened to recollect her.

MRS. SOLNESS.

Miss Wangel was up long ago.

SOLNESS.

Oh, was she ?

MRS. SOLNESS.

When I went in to see her, she was busy putting her things in order.

> [*She goes in front of the mirror and slowly begins to put on her hat.*

SOLNESS.

[*After a short pause.*] So we've found a use for one of our nurseries after all, Aline.

MRS. SOLNESS.

Yes, we have.

SOLNESS.

That seems to me better than to have them all standing empty.

MRS. SOLNESS.

That emptiness is dreadful; you're right there.

SOLNESS.

[*Closes the portfolio, rises and approaches her.*] You'll find that we shall get on far better after this, Aline. Things will be more comfortable. Life will be easier—especially for *you.*

MRS. SOLNESS.

[*Looks at him.*] After this?

SOLNESS.

Yes, believe me, Aline——

MRS. SOLNESS.

Do you mean—because *she* has come here?

SOLNESS.

[*Checking himself.*] I mean, of course—when once we've moved into the new house.

MRS. SOLNESS.

[*Takes her cloak.*] Ah, do you think so, Halvard? Will it be better then?

SOLNESS.

I can't think otherwise. And surely you think so too?

MRS. SOLNESS.

I think nothing at all about the new house.

SOLNESS.

[*Cast down.*] It's hard for me to hear you say that; for you know it's mainly for your sake that I've built it. [*He offers to help her on with her cloak.*

MRS. SOLNESS.

[*Evades him.*] The fact is, you do far too much for my sake.

SOLNESS.

[*With a certain vehemence.*] No, no, you really mustn't say that, Aline. I can't bear to hear you say such things.

MRS. SOLNESS.

Very well, then I won't say it, Halvard.

SOLNESS.

But I stick to what *I* said. You'll see that things 'll be easier for you in the new place.

MRS. SOLNESS.

Oh heavens—easier for me——!

SOLNESS.

[*Eagerly.*] Yes, indeed they will! You may be quite sure of that! For you see—there'll be so very, very much there that'll remind you of your own home——

MRS. SOLNESS.

The home that used to be father's and mother's—and that was burnt to the ground——

SOLNESS.

[*In a low voice.*] Yes, yes, my poor Aline. That was a terrible blow for you.

MRS. SOLNESS.

[*Breaking out in lamentation.*] You may build as much as ever you like, Halvard—you can never build up again a real home for *me!*

SOLNESS.

[*Crosses the room.*] Well, in Heaven's name, let us talk no more about it then.

MRS. SOLNESS.

We're not in the habit of talking about it. For you always put the thought away from you——

SOLNESS.

[*Stops suddenly and looks at her.*] Do I? And why should I do *that*? Put the thought away from me?

MRS. SOLNESS.

Oh yes, Halvard, I understand very well. You're so anxious to spare me—and to find excuses for me too—as much as ever you can.

SOLNESS.

[*With astonishment in his eyes.*] You! Is it *you*—yourself, that you're talking about, Aline?

MRS. SOLNESS.

Yes, who else should it be but myself?

SOLNESS.

[*Involuntarily, to himself.*] *That* too!

MRS. SOLNESS.

As for the old house, I wouldn't mind so much about that. When once misfortune was in the air—why——

SOLNESS.

Ah, you're right there.   Misfortune will have its
way—as the saying goes.

MRS. SOLNESS.

But it's what came of the fire—the dreadful thing
that followed— ! *That* is the thing ! That, that, that !

SOLNESS.

[*Vehemently.*] Don't think about *that*, Aline.

MRS. SOLNESS.

Ah, that's exactly what I can't help thinking about.
And now, at last, I must speak about it, too ; for I
don't seem able to bear it any longer.   And then
never to be able to forgive myself——

SOLNESS.

[*Vehemently.*] Yourself ?

MRS. SOLNESS.

Yes, for I had duties on both sides—both towards you
and towards the little ones.   I ought to have hardened
myself—not to have let the horror take such hold
upon me, nor the grief for the burning for my home.
[*Wrings her hands.*] Oh, Halvard, if I'd only had the
strength !

SOLNESS.

[*Softly, much moved, comes closer.*] Aline—you must promise me never to think these thoughts any more. Promise me that, dear !

MRS. SOLNESS.

Oh, promise, promise ! One can promise anything.

SOLNESS.

[*Clenches his hands and crosses the room.*] Oh, but this is hopeless, hopeless ! Never a ray of sunlight ! Not so much as a gleam of brightness to light up our home !

MRS. SOLNESS.

This *is* no home, Halvard.

SOLNESS.

Oh no, you may well say that. [*Gloomily.*] And God knows whether you're not right in saying that it will be no better for us in the new house, either.

MRS. SOLNESS.

It will never be any better. Just as empty—just as desolate—there as here.

G

SOLNESS.

[*Vehemently.*] Why in all the world have we built it then ? Can you tell me that ?

MRS. SOLNESS.

No ; you must answer that question for yourself.

SOLNESS.

[*Glances suspiciously at her.*] What do you mean by *that*, Aline ?

MRS. SOLNESS.

What do I mean ?

SOLNESS.

Yes, in the devil's name ! You said it so strangely —as if you had some hidden meaning in it.

MRS. SOLNESS.

No, indeed, I assure you——

SOLNESS.

[*Comes closer.*] Oh, come now—I know what I know. I've both my eyes and my ears about me, Aline— you may depend upon that !

MRS. SOLNESS.

Why, what are you talking about ? What is it ?

SOLNESS.

[*Places himself in front of her.*] Do you mean to say you don't find a kind of lurking, hidden meaning in the most innocent word I happen to say?

MRS. SOLNESS.

I, do you say? *I* do that?

SOLNESS.

[*Laughs.*] Ho-ho-ho! It's natural enough, Aline! When you've a sick man on your hands——

MRS. SOLNESS.

[*Anxiously.*] *Sick?* Are you ill, Halvard?

SOLNESS.

[*Violently.*] A half-mad man then! A crazy man! Call me what you will.

MRS. SOLNESS.

[*Feels gropingly for a chair and sits down.*] Halvard —for God's sake——

SOLNESS.

But you're wrong, both you and the doctor. That's not what's the matter with me.

[*He walks up and down the room.* MRS. SOL-
NESS *follows him anxiously with her eyes.
Finally he goes up to her.*

SOLNESS.

[*Calmly.*] In reality there's nothing whatever wrong
with me.

MRS. SOLNESS.

No, there isn't, is there ?   But then what is it that
troubles you so ?

SOLNESS.

Why this, that I often feel ready to sink under this
terrible burden of debt——

MRS. SOLNESS.

Debt, do you say ?   But you owe no one anything,
Halvard !

SOLNESS.

[*Softly, with emotion.*]   I owe a boundless debt to
you—to you—to you, Aline.

MRS. SOLNESS.

[*Rises slowly.*]   What is behind all this ?   You may
just as well tell me at once.

SOLNESS

But there *is* nothing behind it. I've never done you any wrong—not wittingly and wilfully, at any rate. And yet—and yet it seems as though a crushing debt rested upon me and weighed me down.

MRS. SOLNESS.

A debt to me ?

SOLNESS.

Chiefly to you.

MRS. SOLNESS.

Then you are—ill after all, Halvard.

SOLNESS.

[*Gloomily.*] I suppose I must be—or not far from it. [*Looks towards the door to the right, which is opened at this moment.*] Ah ! now it grows lighter.

HILDA WANGEL *comes in. She has made some alterations in her dress, and let down her skirt.*

HILDA.

Good morning, Mr. Solness !

SOLNESS.

[*Nods.*] Slept well ?

HILDA.

Quite deliciously ! As if in a cradle. Oh—I lay
and stretched myself like—like a princess !

SOLNESS.

Smiles a little.] You were thoroughly comfortable
hen ?

HILDA.

I should think so.

SOLNESS.

And no doubt you dreamed, too.

HILDA.

Yes, I did. But *that* was horrid.

SOLNESS.

Indeed ?

HILDA.

Yes, for I dreamed I was falling over a frightfully
high, sheer precipice. Do you never have that kind
of dream ?

SOLNESS.

Oh yes—now and then——

HILDA.

It's tremendously thrilling—when you fall and
fall——

SOLNESS.

It seems to make one's blood run cold.

HILDA.

Do you draw your legs up under you while you're falling ?

SOLNESS.

Yes, as high as ever I can.

HILDA.

So do I.

MRS. SOLNESS.

[*Takes her parasol.*] I must go into town now, Halvard. [*To* HILDA.] And I'll try to get one or two things that may be of use to you.

HILDA.

[*Making a motion to throw her arms round her neck.*] Oh, you dear, sweet Mrs. Solness ! You're really much too kind to me ! Frightfully kind——

MRS. SOLNESS.

[*Deprecatingly, freeing herself.*] Oh, far from it. It's only my duty, so I'm very glad to do it.

HILDA.

[*Offended, pouts.*] But really, I think I'm quite fit
to be seen in the streets—now that I've put my dress
to rights. Or do you think I'm not?

MRS. SOLNESS.

To tell you the truth, I think people would stare
at you a little.

HILDA.

[*Contemptuously.*] Pooh! Is that all? That only
amuses me.

SOLNESS.

[*With suppressed ill-humour.*] Yes, but people might
take it into their heads that *you* were mad too, you
see.

HILDA.

Mad? Are there so many mad people here in
town, then?

SOLNESS.

[*Points to his own forehead.*] Here you see *one* at
all events.

HILDA.

You—Mr. Solness!

MRS. SOLNESS.

Oh, don't talk like that, my dear Halvard!

SOLNESS.

Haven't you noticed *that* yet?

HILDA.

No, I certainly haven't. [*Reflects and laughs a little.*] And yet—perhaps in one single thing.

SOLNESS.

Ah, do you hear *that*, Aline?

MRS. SOLNESS.

What is that one single thing, Miss Wangel?

HILDA.

No, I won't say.

SOLNESS.

Oh yes, do!

HILDA.

No thanks—I'm not so mad as all that.

MRS. SOLNESS.

When you and Miss Wangel are alone, I daresay she'll tell you, Halvard.

SOLNESS.

Ah—you think she will?

MRS. SOLNESS.

Oh yes, certainly. For you've known her so well in the past. Ever since she was a child—you tell me.

[*She goes out by the door on the left.*

HILDA.

[*After a little while.*] Does your wife dislike me very much?

SOLNESS.

Did you think you noticed anything of the kind?

HILDA.

Didn't you notice it yourself?

SOLNESS.

[*Evasively.*] Aline has become exceedingly shy with strangers of late years.

HILDA.

Has she really?

SOLNESS.

But if only you could get to know her thoroughly —Ah, she's so nice—and so kind—and so good at heart.

HILDA.

[*Impatiently.*] But if she's all that—what made her say that about her duty?

SOLNESS.

Her duty?

HILDA.

She said that she would go out and buy something for me, because it was her *duty*. Oh I can't bear that ugly, horrid word!

SOLNESS.

Why not?

HILDA.

It sounds so cold, and sharp, and stinging. Duty—duty—duty. Don't *you* think so, too? Doesn't it seem to sting you?

SOLNESS.

H'm—haven't thought much about it.

HILDA.

Yes, it does. And if she's so nice—as you say she is—why should she talk in that way?

SOLNESS.

But, good Lord, what would you have had her say, then?

HILDA.

She might have said she would do it because she had taken a tremendous fancy to me. She might have said something like that—something really warm and cordial, you understand.

SOLNESS.

[*Looks at her.*] Is that how you'd like to have it ?

HILDA.

Yes, precisely. [*She wanders about the room, stops at the bookcase and looks at the books.*] What a lot of books you have.

SOLNESS.

Yes, I've got together a good many.

HILDA.

Do you read them all, too ?

SOLNESS.

I used to try to.   Do you read much ?

HILDA.

No, never ! I've given it up.   For it all seems so irrelevant.

SOLNESS.

That's just my feeling.

> [HILDA *wanders about a little, stops at the small table, opens the portfolio and turns over the contents.*

HILDA.

Are all these drawings yours ?

SOLNESS.

No, they're drawn by a young man whom I employ to help me.

HILDA.

Some one you've taught ?

SOLNESS.

Oh yes, no doubt he's learnt something from me, too.

HILDA.

[*Sits down.*] Then I suppose he's very clever. [*Looks at a drawing.*] Isn't he ?

SOLNESS.

Oh, he's not bad.   For *my* purpose——

HILDA.

Oh yes—I'm sure he's frightfully clever.

SOLNESS.

Do you think you can see that in the drawings ?

HILDA.

Pooh—these scrawlings !   But if he's been learning from *you*——

SOLNESS.

Oh, as far as that goes——there are plenty of
people here that have learnt from *me*, and have
come to little enough for all that.

HILDA.

[*Looks at him and shakes her head.*] No, I can't
for the life of me understand how you can be so
stupid.

SOLNESS.

Stupid? Do you think I'm so very stupid?

HILDA.

Yes, I do indeed. If you're content to go about
here teaching all these people——

SOLNESS.

[*With a slight start.*] Well, and why not?

HILDA.

[*Rises, half serious, half-laughing.*] No indeed, Mr.
Solness! What can be the good of that? No one
but yourself should be allowed to build. You should
stand quite alone—do it all yourself. Now you know
it.

SOLNESS.

[*Involuntarily.*] Hilda——!

HILDA.

Well!

SOLNESS.

How in the world did that come into your head?

HILDA.

Do you think I'm so very far wrong then?

SOLNESS.

No, that's not what I mean. But now I'll tell you something.

HILDA.

Well?

SOLNESS.

I keep on—incessantly—in silence and alone—brooding on that very thought.

HILDA.

Yes, that seems to me perfectly natural.

SOLNESS.

[*Looks somewhat searchingly at her.*] Perhaps you've already noticed it?

HILDA.

No, indeed I haven't.

SOLNESS.

But just now—when you said you thought I was—
off my balance ? In one thing, you said——

HILDA.

Oh, I was thinking of something quite different.

SOLNESS.

What was it ?

HILDA.

I'm not going to tell you.

SOLNESS.

[*Crosses the room.*] Well, well—as you please
[*Stops at the bow-window.*] Come here and I'll show
you something.

HILDA.

[*Approaching.*] What is it ?

SOLNESS.

Do you see—over there in the garden——?

HILDA.

Yes ?

SOLNESS.

[*Points.*] Right above the great quarry——?

HILDA.

That new house, you mean?

SOLNESS.

The one that's being built, yes. Almost finished.

HILDA.

It seems to have a very high tower.

SOLNESS.
The scaffolding is still up.

HILDA.

Is that your new house?

SOLNESS.
Yes.

HILDA.

The house you're soon going to move into?

SOLNESS.
Yes.

HILDA.

[*Looks at him.*] Are there nurseries in *that* house, too?

SOLNESS.

Three, as there are here.

H

HILDA.

And no child.

SOLNESS

And there never will be one.

HILDA.

[*With a half-smile.*] Well, isn't it just as I said—— ?

SOLNESS.

That—— ?

HILDA.

That you *are* a little—a little mad after all.

SOLNESS.

Was that what you were thinking of ?

HILDA.

Yes, of all the empty nurseries I slept in.

SOLNESS.

[*Lowers his voice.*] We *have* had children—Aline and I.

HILDA.

[*Looks eagerly at him.*] Have you—— ?

SOLNESS.

Two little boys. They were of the same age.

HILDA.

Twins, then.

SOLNESS.

Yes, twins. It's eleven or twelve years ago now.

HILDA.

[*Cautiously.*] And so both of them——? You have lost both the twins, then?

SOLNESS.

[*With quiet emotion.*] We only kept them about three weeks. Or scarcely so much. [*Bursts forth.*] Oh, Hilda, I can't tell you what a good thing it is for me that you have come! For now at last I have some one I can talk to!

HILDA.

Can't you talk to—to *her*, too?

SOLNESS.

Not about this. Not as I want to talk and must talk. [*Gloomily.*] And not about so many other things, too.

HILDA.

[*In a subdued voice.*] Was that all you meant when you said you needed me?

SOLNESS.

That was mainly what I meant—at all events, yesterday. For to-day I'm not so sure.—[*Breaking off.*] Come here and let us sit down, Hilda. Sit there on the sofa—so that you can look into the garden. [HILDA *seats herself in the corner of the sofa.* SOLNESS *brings a chair closer.*] Would you like to hear about it?

HILDA.

Yes, I shall love to sit and listen to you.

SOLNESS

[*Sits down.*] Then I'll tell you all about it.

HILDA.

Now I can see both the garden and you, Mr. Solness. So now, tell away! Go on!

SOLNESS.

[*Points towards the bow-window.*] Out there on the rising ground—where you see the new house——

HILDA.

Yes.

SOLNESS.

Aline and I lived there in the first years of our married life. There was an old house up there that had belonged to her mother; and we inherited it, and the whole of the great garden with it.

HILDA.

Was there a tower on *that* house, too?

SOLNESS.

No, nothing of the kind. From the outside it looked like a great, dark, ugly wooden box; but, all the same, it was snug and comfortable enough inside.

HILDA.

Then did you pull down the ramshackle old place?

SOLNESS.

No, it was burnt down.

HILDA.

The whole of it?

SOLNESS.

Yes.

HILDA.

Was that a great misfortune for you?

SOLNESS.

That depends on how you look at it. As a builder, the fire was the making of me——

HILDA.

Well, but——?

SOLNESS.

It was just after the birth of the two little boys.

HILDA.

The poor little twins, yes.

SOLNESS.

They came healthy and bonny into the world. And they were growing too—you could see the difference from day to day.

HILDA.

Little children do grow quickly at first.

SOLNESS.

It was the prettiest sight in the world to see Aline lying with the two of them in her arms. But then came the night of the fire——

HILDA.

[*Excitedly.*] What happened? Do tell me! Was any one burnt?

SOLNESS.

No, not that. Every one got safe and sound out of the house——

HILDA.

Well, and what then ?

SOLNESS.

The fright had shaken Aline terribly. The alarm—the escape—the break-neck hurry—and then the ice-cold night air—for they had to be carried out just as they lay—both she and the little ones——

HILDA.

Was it too much for them ?

SOLNESS.

Oh no, *they* stood it well enough. But Aline fell into a fever, and it affected her milk. She would insist on nursing them herself; because it was her duty, she said. And both our little boys, they— [*clenching his hands*] they—oh !

HILDA.

They didn't get over *that ?*

SOLNESS.

No, *that* they didn't get over.   That was how we lost them.

HILDA.

It must have been terribly hard for you.

SOLNESS.

Hard enough for me; but ten times harder for Aline.   [*Clenching his hands in suppressed fury.*]   Oh, that such things should be allowed to happen here on earth!   [*Shortly and firmly.*]   From the day I lost them, I had no heart for building churches.

HILDA.

Didn't you like building the church-tower in our town ?

SOLNESS.

I didn't like it.   I know how free and happy I felt when that tower was finished.

HILDA.

I know that, too.

SOLNESS.

And now I shall never—never build anything of that sort again !   Neither churches nor church-towers.

HILDA.

[*Nods slowly.*] Nothing but houses for people to live in.

SOLNESS.

Homes for human beings, Hilda.

HILDA.

But homes with high towers and pinnacles upon them.

SOLNESS.

If possible. [*Adopts a lighter tone.*] Well, you·see, as I said, that fire was the making of me—as a builder, I mean.

HILDA.

Why don't you call yourself an architect, like the others?

SOLNESS.

I haven't been systematically enough taught for that. Most of what I know, I've found out for myself.

HILDA.

But you succeeded all the same.

SOLNESS.

Yes, thanks to the fire. I laid out almost the whole of the garden in villa-lots; and *there* I was able to build entirely after my own heart. So I came to the front with a rush.

HILDA.

[*Looks keenly at him.*] You must surely be a very happy man—situated as you are.

SOLNESS.

[*Gloomily.*] Happy? Do *you* say that, too—like all the rest of them?

HILDA.

Yes, I should say you must be. If you could only get the two little children out of your head——

SOLNESS.

[*Slowly.*] The two little children—they're not so easy to forget, Hilda.

HILDA.

[*Somewhat uncertainly.*] Do you still feel their loss so much—after all these years?

SOLNESS.

[*Looks fixedly at her, without replying.*] A happy man, you said——

HILDA.

Well now, *are* you not happy—in other respects?

SOLNESS.

[*Continues to look at her.*] When I told you all this about the fire—h'm——

HILDA.

Well?

SOLNESS.

Was there not one special thought that you—that you seized upon?

HILDA.

[*Reflects in vain.*] No. What thought should that be?

SOLNESS.

[*With subdued emphasis.*] It was simply and solely by that fire that I was enabled to build homes for human beings. Cosy, comfortable, bright homes, where father and mother and the whole troop of children can live in safety and gladness, feeling what a happy thing it is to be alive in the world—and most of all to belong to each other—in great things and in small.

HILDA.

[*Ardently.*] Well, and isn't it a great happiness for you to be able to build such beautiful homes?

SOLNESS.

The price, Hilda! The terrible price I had to pay for it!

HILDA.

But can you *never* get over that?

SOLNESS,

No. That I might build homes for others, I had to forego—to forego for all time—the home that might have been my own. I mean a home for a troop of children—and for father and mother, too.

HILDA

[*Cautiously.*] But need you have done that? For all time, you say?

SOLNESS.

[*Nods slowly.*] *That* was the price of this happiness that people talk about. [*Breathes heavily.*] This happiness—h'm—this happiness was not to be bought any cheaper, Hilda.

HILDA.

[*As before.*] But may it not come right even yet?

SOLNESS.

Never in this world—never. That is another consequence of the fire—and of Aline's illness afterwards.

HILDA.

[*Looks at him with an indefinable expression.*] And yet you build all these nurseries?

SOLNESS.

[*Seriously.*] Have you never noticed, Hilda, how the impossible—how it seems to beckon and cry aloud to one?

HILDA.

[*Reflecting.*] The impossible? [*With animation.*] Yes, indeed! Is that how *you* feel too?

SOLNESS.

Yes, I do.

HILDA.

Then there must be—a little of the troll in you too?

SOLNESS.

Why of the troll?

HILDA.

What would *you* call it, then?

SOLNESS.

[*Rises.*] Well, well, perhaps you're right. [*Vehemently.*] But how can I help turning into a troll, when this is how it always goes with me in everything--in everything!

HILDA.

How do you mean?

SOLNESS.

[*Speaking low, with inward emotion.*] Mark what I say to you, Hilda. All that I have succeeded in doing, building, creating—all the beauty, security, cheerful comfort—ay, and magnificence too—[*Clenches his hands*]—oh, isn't it terrible even to think of——!

HILDA.

What is so terrible?

SOLNESS.

That all this I have to make up for, to pay for— not in money,. but in human happiness. And not with my own happiness only, but with other people's too. Yes, yes, do you see that, Hilda? That is the price which my position as an artist has cost me—and others. And every single day I have to look on while the price is paid for me anew. Over again, and over again—and over again for ever!

HILDA.

[*Rises and looks steadily at him.*] Now I can see you're thinking of—of *her.*

SOLNESS.

Yes, mainly of Aline. For Aline—she, too, had her vocation in life, just as much as I had mine. [*His voice quivers.*] But her vocation has had to be stunted, and crushed, and shattered—in order 'that mine might force its way to—to a sort of great victory. For you must know that Aline—she, too, had a turn for building.

HILDA.

She? For building?

SOLNESS.

[*Shakes his head.*] Not houses, and towers, and spires—not such things as I work away at——

HILDA.

Well, but *what,* then?

SOLNESS.

[*Softly, with emotion.*] For building up the souls of little children, Hilda. For building up children's souls in perfect balance, and in noble and beautiful forms. For enabling them to soar up into erect and full-grown human souls. That was Aline's talent. And there it all lies now—unused, and unusable for ever—of no earthly service to any one—just like the ruins left by a fire.

HILDA.

Yes, but even if this were so——

SOLNESS.

It *is* so! It *is* so! I know it!

HILDA.

Well, but in any case it's not *your* fault.

SOLNESS.

[*Fixes his eyes on her, and nods slowly.*] Ah, *that* is the great, the terrible question. *That* is the doubt that's gnawing me—night and day.

HILDA.

That ?

SOLNESS.

Yes.   Suppose the fault *was* mine—in a certain sense.

HILDA.

Your fault !   The fire !

SOLNESS.

All of it ; the whole thing.   And yet, perhaps—I mayn't have had anything to do with it.

HILDA.

[*Looks at him with a troubled expression.*]   Oh, Mr. Solness, if you can talk like that, I'm afraid you must be—ill, after all.

SOLNESS.

H'm—I don't think I shall ever be of quite sound mind on that point.

RAGNAR BROVIK *cautiously opens the little door in the left-hand corner.* HILDA *comes forward.*

RAGNAR.

[*When he sees* HILDA.]   Oh.   I beg pardon, Mr. Solness——   [*He makes a movement to withdraw.*

I

SOLNESS.

No, no, don't go.   Let's get it over.

RAGNAR.

Oh, yes—if only we could.

SOLNESS.

I hear your father is no better ?

RAGNAR.

Father is fast growing weaker—and therefore I beg
and implore you to write a few kind words for me
on one of the plans !   Something for father to read
before he——

SOLNESS.

[*Vehemently.*] I won't hear anything more about
those drawings of yours !

RAGNAR.

Have you looked at them ?

SOLNESS.

Yes, I have.

RAGNAR.

And they're good for nothing? And *I* am good for nothing, too?

SOLNESS.

[*Evasively.*] Stay here with me, Ragnar. You shall have everything your own way. And then you can marry Kaia, and live at your ease—and—and happily too, who knows? Only don't think of building on your own account.

RAGNAR.

Well, well, then I must go home and tell father what you say—I promised I would. *Is* this what I am to tell father—before he dies?

SOLNESS.

[*With a groan.*] Oh tell him—tell him what you will, for me. Best to say nothing at all to him! [*With a sudden outburst.*] I *cannot* do anything else, Ragnar!

RAGNAR.

May I have the drawings to take with me?

SOLNESS.

Yes, take them—take them by all means! They're lying there on the table.

RAGNAR.

[*Goes to the table.*] Thanks.

HILDA.

[*Puts her hand on the portfolio.*] No, no; leave them here.

SOLNESS.

Why ?

HILDA.

Because I want to look at them, too

SOLNESS.

But you *have* been—— [*To* RAGNAR.] Well, leave them here, then.

RAGNAR.

Very well.

SOLNESS

And go home at once to your father.

RAGNAR.

Yes, I suppose I must.

SOLNESS.

[*As if in desperation.*] Ragnar—you *must* not ask me to do what's beyond my power ! Do you hear, Ragnar ? You *must* not !

RAGNAR.

No, no. I beg your pardon——

[*He bows, and goes out by the corner door.*
HILDA *goes over and sits down on a chair
near the mirror.*

HILDA.

[*Looks angrily at* SOLNESS.] That was a very ugly
thing to do.

SOLNESS.

Do *you* think so, too?

HILDA.

Yes, it was horribly ugly—and hard and bad and
cruel as well.

SOLNESS.

Oh, you don't understand my position.

HILDA.

All the same——. No, you oughtn't to be like
that.

SOLNESS.

You said yourself, only just now, that no one but
I ought to be allowed to build.

HILDA.

I may say such things—but *you* mayn't.

SOLNESS.

I most of all, surely, who have paid so dear for my position.

HILDA.

Oh yes—with what you call domestic comfort— and that sort of thing.

SOLNESS.

And with my peace of soul into the bargain.

HILDA.

[*Rising.*] Peace of soul! [*With feeling.*] Yes, yes, you're right in that! Poor Mr. Solness—you fancy that——

SOLNESS.

[*With a quiet, chuckling laugh.*] Just sit down again, Hilda, and I'll tell you something funny.

HILDA.

[*Sits down; with intent interest.*] Well?

SOLNESS.

It sounds such a ludicrous little thing; for, you see, the whole story turns upon nothing but a crack in a chimney.

HILDA.

No more than that ?

SOLNESS.

No, not to begin with.

[*He moves a chair nearer to* HILDA *and sits down.*

HILDA.

[*Impatiently, taps on her knee.*] Well, now for the crack in the chimney !

SOLNESS.

I had noticed the split in the flue long, long before the fire. Every time I went up into the attic, I looked to see if it was still there.

HILDA.

And it *was ?*

SOLNESS.

Yes ; for no one else knew about it.

HILDA.

And you said nothing ?

SOLNESS.

Nothing.

HILDA.

And didn't think of repairing the flue either?

SOLNESS.

Oh yes, I thought about it—but never got any further. Every time I intended to set to work, it seemed just as if a hand held me back. Not to-day, I thought—to-morrow; and nothing ever came of it.

HILDA.

But why did you keep putting it off like that?

SOLNESS.

Because I was revolving something in my mind. [*Slowly, and in a low voice.*] Through that little black crack in the chimney I might, perhaps, force my way upwards—as a builder.

HILDA.

[*Looking straight in front of her.*] That must have been thrilling.

SOLNESS.

Almost irresistible—quite irresistible. For at that time it appeared to me a perfectly simple and straight-forward matter. I would have had it happen in the winter-time—a little before midday. I was to be out driving Aline in the sleigh. The servants at home would have made a huge fire in the stove.

HILDA.

For, of course, it was to be bitterly cold that day ?

SOLNESS.

Rather biting, yes—and they would want Aline to find it thoroughly snug and warm when she came home.

HILDA.

I suppose she's very chilly by nature ?

SOLNESS.

She *is*. And as we drove home, we were to see the smoke.

HILDA.

Only the smoke?

SOLNESS.

The smoke first. But when we came up to the garden gate, the whole of the old timber-box was to be a rolling mass of flames.—That's how I wanted it to be, you see.

HILDA.

Oh why, *why* couldn't it have happened so !

SOLNESS.

You may well say that, Hilda.

HILDA.

Well, but now listen, Mr. Solness. Are you perfectly certain that the fire was caused by that little crack in the chimney ?

SOLNESS.

No, on the contrary—I'm perfectly certain that the crack in the chimney had nothing whatever to do with the fire.

HILDA.

What !

SOLNESS.

It has been clearly ascertained that the fire broke out in a clothes-cupboard—in a totally different part of the house.

HILDA.

Then what's all this nonsense you're talking about the crack in the chimney ?

SOLNESS.

May I go on talking to you a little, Hilda ?

HILDA.

Yes, if you'll only talk sensibly——

SOLNESS.

I'll try to.   [*He moves his chair nearer.*

HILDA.

Out with it then, Mr. Solness.

SOLNESS.

[*Confidentially.*] Don't you agree with me, Hilda, that there exist special, chosen people who have been endowed with the power and faculty of *desiring* a thing, *craving* for a thing, *willing* a thing—so persistently and so—so inexorably—that at last it *has* to happen? Don't you believe that?

HILDA.

[*With an indefinable expression in her eyes.*] If that is so, we shall see, one of these days, whether *I* am one of the chosen.

SOLNESS.

It's not one's self alone that can do such great things. Oh, no—the helpers and the servers—they must do their part too, if it's to be of any good But they never come of themselves. One has to call upon them very persistently—inwardly, you understand.

HILDA.

What are these helpers and servers?

SOLNESS.

Oh, we can talk about that some other time. For the present, let us keep to this business of the fire.

HILDA.

Don't you think the fire would have happened all the same—even if you hadn't wished for it?

SOLNESS.

If the house had been old Knut Brovik's, it would never have burnt down so conveniently for *him*. I'm sure of that; for he doesn't know how to call for the helpers—no, nor for the servers, either. [*Rises in agitation.*] So you see, Hilda—it's my fault, after all, that the lives of the two little boys had to be sacrificed. And do you think it isn't my fault, too, that Aline has never been the woman she should and might have been—and that she most longed to be?

HILDA.

Yes, but if it's all the work of those helpers and servers——?

SOLNESS.

Who called for the helpers and servers? It was *I !* And they came and obeyed my will. [*In increasing excitement.*] *That's* what good people call having the luck on your side; but I must tell you what this sort of luck feels like! It feels like a great raw place here on my breast. And the helpers and servers keep on flaying pieces of skin off other people in order to close my sore. But still the sore is not healed—never, never! Oh, if you knew how it can sometimes gnaw and burn.

HILDA.

[*Looks attentively at him.*] You *are* ill, Mr. Solness. Very ill, I almost think.

SOLNESS.

Say *mad;* for that's what you mean.

HILDA.

No, I don't think there's much amiss with your intellect.

SOLNESS.

With *what*, then? Out with it!

HILDA.

I wonder whether you weren't sent into the world with a sickly conscience.

SOLNESS.

A sickly conscience ? What devilry is that ?

HILDA.

I mean that your conscience is feeble—too delicately built, as it were—hasn't strength to take a grip of things—to lift and bear what's heavy.

SOLNESS.

[*Growls.*] H'm ! May I ask, then, what sort of a conscience one ought to have ?

HILDA.

I should like *your* conscience to be thoroughly robust.

SOLNESS.

Indeed ? Robust, eh ? Is your own conscience robust ?

HILDA.

Yes, I think it is. I've never noticed that it wasn't.

SOLNESS.

It hasn't been put very severely to the test, I should think.

HILDA.

[*With a quivering of the lips.*] Oh, it wasn't such a simple matter to leave father—I'm so awfully fond of him.

SOLNESS.

Dear me! for a month or two——

HILDA.

I don't think I shall ever go home again.

SOLNESS.

Never? Then why did you leave him?

HILDA.

[*Half-seriously, half-banteringly.*] Have you forgotten again that the ten years are up?

SOLNESS.

Oh nonsense. Was anything wrong at home? Eh?

HILDA.

[*Quite seriously.*] It *was* this something within me that drove and spurred me here—and allured and attracted me, too.

SOLNESS.

[*Eagerly.*] There we have it! There we have it, Hilda! There's a troll in you too, as in me. For it's the troll in one, you see—it's *that* that calls to the powers outside us. And then you *must* give in— whether you will or no.

HILDA.

I almost think you're right, Mr. Solness.

SOLNESS.

[*Walks about the room.*] Oh, there are devils in-numerable abroad in the world, Hilda, that one never *sees!*

HILDA.

Devils, too?

SOLNESS.

[*Stops.*] Good devils and bad devils; light-haired devils and black-haired devils. If only you could always tell whether it's the light or the dark ones that have got hold of you! [*Paces about.*] Ho, ho! Then it would be simple enough!

HILDA.

[*Follows him with her eyes.*] Or if one had a really vigorous, radiantly healthy conscience—so that one *dared* to do what one *would.*

SOLNESS.

[*Stops beside the console table.*] I believe, now, that most people are just as puny creatures as I am in this respect.

HILDA.

I shouldn't wonder.

SOLNESS.

[*Leaning against the table.*] In the sagas——. Have you read any of the old sagas?

HILDA.

Oh yes! When I used to read books, I——

SOLNESS.

In the sagas you read about vikings, who sailed to foreign lands, and plundered and burned and killed men——

HILDA

And carried off women——

SOLNESS.

——and kept them in captivity——

HILDA.

——took them home in their ships——

K

SOLNESS.

——and behaved to them like—like the very worst
of trolls.

HILDA.

[*Looks straight before her with a half-veiled look.*] I
think *that* must have been thrilling.

SOLNESS.

[*With a short, deep laugh.*] To carry off women,
eh ?

HILDA.

To *be* carried off.

SOLNESS.

[*Looks at her a moment.*] Oh, indeed.

HILDA.

[*As if breaking the thread of conversation.*] But
what made you speak of these vikings, Mr. Solness ?

SOLNESS.

Because *those* fellows must have had robust con-
sciences, if you like ! When they got home again,
they could eat and drink, and be as happy as children. And the women, too ! They often wouldn't
leave them on any account. Can you understand
that, Hilda ?

HILDA.

Those women I can understand exceedingly well.

SOLNESS.

Oho ! Perhaps you could do the same yourself ?

HILDA.

Why not ?

SOLNESS.

Live—of your own free will—with a ruffian like
that ?

HILDA.

If it was a ruffian I had come to love——·

SOLNESS.

Could you come to love a man like that ?

HILDA.

Good heavens, you know very well one can't choose
whom one's going to love.

SOLNESS.

[*Looks meditatively at her.*] Oh no, I suppose it's
the troll within one that's responsible for that.

HILDA.

[*Half-laughing.*] And all those blessed devils, that *you* know so well—both the light-haired and the dark-haired ones.

SOLNESS.

[*Quietly and warmly.*] Then I hope with all my heart that the devils will choose carefully for you, Hilda.

HILDA.

For me they *have* chosen already—once and for all.

SOLNESS.

[*Looks earnestly at her.*] Hilda, you are like a wild bird of the woods.

HILDA.

Far from it.   I don't hide myself away under the bushes.

SOLNESS.

No, no.   There's rather something of the bird of prey in you.

HILDA.

That's nearer it—perhaps. [*Very vehemently.*] And why not a bird of prey? Why shouldn't *I* go a-hunting—I, as well as the rest ? Carry off the prey I want—if I can only get my claws into it, and have my own way with it.

SOLNESS.

Hilda—do you know what you are?

HILDA.

Yes, I suppose I'm a strange sort of bird.

SOLNESS.

No. You are like a dawning day. When I look at you, I seem to be looking towards the sunrise.

HILDA.

Tell me, Mr. Solness—are you certain that you've never called me to you?—Inwardly, you know?

SOLNESS.

[*Softly and slowly.*] I almost think I must have.

HILDA.

What did you want with me?

SOLNESS.

You are the younger generation, Hilda.

HILDA.

[*Smiles.*] That younger generation that you're so afraid of.

SOLNESS.

[*Nods slowly.*] And which, in my heart, I yearn towards so deeply.

HILDA *rises, goes to the little table, and fetches* RAGNAR BROVIK'S *portfolio.*

HILDA.

[*Holds out the portfolio to him.*] We were talking of these drawings——

SOLNESS.

[*Shortly, waving them away.*] Put those things away! I've seen enough of them.

HILDA.

Yes, but you have to write your approval on them.

SOLNESS.

Write my approval on them? Never!

HILDA.

But the poor old man is lying at death's door! Can't you give him and his son this pleasure before they're parted? And perhaps he might get the commission to carry them out, too.

SOLNESS.

Yes, that's just what he would get. He's made sure of that—has my fine gentleman !

HILDA.

Then, good heavens—if that's so—can't you tell the least little bit of a lie for once ?

SOLNESS.

A lie ? [*Raging.*] Hilda—take those devil's drawings out of my sight !

HILDA.

[*Draws the portfolio a little nearer to herself.*] Well well, well—don't bite me.—You talk of trolls—but I think you go on like a troll yourself. [*Looks round.*] Where do you keep your pen and ink ?

SOLNESS.

There's nothing of the sort in here.

HILDA.

[*Goes towards the door.*] But in the office where that young lady is——

SOLNESS.

Stay where you are, Hilda !—I ought to tell a lie, you say. Oh yes, for the sake of his old father I might well do that—for in my time I've crushed him, trodden him under foot——

HILDA.

Him, too ?

SOLNESS.

I needed room for myself. But this Ragnar—he must on no account be allowed to come to the front.

HILDA.

Poor fellow, there's surely no fear of that. If he has nothing in him——

SOLNESS.

[*Comes closer, looks at her, and whispers.*] If Ragnar Brovik comes to the front he will strike *me* to the earth. Crush me—as I crushed his father.

HILDA.

Crush you ? Has he the ability for that ?

SOLNESS.

Yes, you may depend upon it *he* has the ability ! He is the younger generation that stands ready to knock at my door— to make an end of Halvard Solness.

HILDA.

[*Looks at him with quiet reproach.*] And yet you would bar him out. Fie, Mr. Solness!

SOLNESS.

The fight I have been fighting has cost heart's blood enough.—And I'm afraid, too, that the helpers and servers won't obey me any longer.

HILDA.

Then you must go ahead without them. There's nothing else for it.

SOLNESS.

It's hopeless, Hilda. The luck is bound to turn. A little sooner or a little later. Retribution is inexorable.

HILDA.

[*In distress, putting her hands over her ears.*] Don't talk like that! Do you want to kill me? To take from me what is more than my life?

SOLNESS.

And what is that?

HILDA.

The longing to see you great. To see you, with a wreath in your hand, high, high up upon a church-tower. [*Calm again.*] Come, out with your pencil now. You must have a pencil about you!

SOLNESS.

[*Takes out his pocket-book.*] I have one here.

HILDA.

[*Puts the portfolio on the sofa-table.*] Very well. Now let us two sit down here, Mr. Solness. [SOLNESS *seats himself at the table,* HILDA *behind him, leaning over the back of the chair.*] And now we'll write on the drawings. We must write very, very nicely and cordially—for this horrid Ruar—or whatever his name is.

SOLNESS.

[*Writes a few words, turns his head and looks at her.*] Tell me one thing, Hilda.

HILDA.

Yes!

SOLNESS.

If you've been waiting for me all these ten years——

HILDA.

What then ?

SOLNESS.

Why have you never written to me? Then I could have answered you.

HILDA.

[*Hastily.*] No, no, no! That was just what I didn't want.

SOLNESS.

Why not ?

HILDA.

I was afraid the whole thing might fall to pieces.— But we were going to write on the drawings, Mr. Solness.

SOLNESS.

So we were.

HILDA.

[*Bends forward and looks over his shoulder while he writes.*] Mind now ! kindly and cordially ! Oh how I hate—how I hate this Ruald——

SOLNESS.

[*Writing.*] Have you never really cared for any one, Hilda?

HILDA.

[*Harshly.*] What do you say?

SOLNESS.

Have you never cared for any one?

HILDA.

For any one else, I suppose you mean?

SOLNESS.

[*Looks up at her.*] For any one else, yes. Have you never? In all these ten years? Never?

HILDA.

Oh yes, now and then. When I was perfectly furious with you for not coming.

SOLNESS.

Then you did take an interest in other people, too?

HILDA.

A little bit—for a week or so. Good heavens, Mr. Solness, you surely know how such things come about.

SOLNESS.

Hilda—what is it you've come for?

HILDA.

Don't waste time in talking. The poor old man might go and die in the meantime.

SOLNESS.

Answer me, Hilda. What do you want of me?

HILDA.

I want my kingdom.

SOLNESS.

H'm——

> [*He gives a rapid glance towards the door on the left, and then goes on writing on the drawings. At the same moment* MRS. SOLNESS *enters ; she has some packages in her hand.*

MRS. SOLNESS.

Here are a few things I've got for you, Miss Wangel. The large parcels will be sent later on.

HILDA.

Oh, how very, very kind of you.

MRS. SOLNESS.

Only my simple duty. Nothing more than that.

SOLNESS.

[*Reading over what he has written.*] Aline!

MRS. SOLNESS.

Yes!

SOLNESS.

Did you notice whether the—the book-keeper was out there?

MRS. SOLNESS.

Yes, of course, *she* was there.

SOLNESS.

[*Puts the drawings in the portfolio.*] H'm——

MRS. SOLNESS.

She was standing at the desk, as she always is—when *I* go through the room.

SOLNESS.

[*Rises.*] Then I'll give this to her, and tell her that——

HILDA.

[*Takes the portfolio from him.*] Oh, no, let me have the pleasure of doing that! [*Goes to the door, but turns.*] What's her name?

SOLNESS.

Her name is Miss Fosli.

HILDA.

Pooh, that sounds so cold. Her Christian name, I mean?

SOLNESS.

Kaia—I believe.

HILDA.

[*Opens the door and calls out.*] Kaia, come in here! Make haste! Mr. Solness wants to speak to you.

KAIA FOSLI *appears at the door.*

KAIA.

[*Looking at him in alarm.*] Here I am.

HILDA.

[*Handing her the portfolio.*] See here, Kaia? You can take these home; Mr. Solness has written on them now.

KAIA.

Oh, at last !

SOLNESS.

Give them to the old man as soon as you can.

KAIA.

I will go straight home with them.

SOLNESS.

Yes, do. Now Ragnar will have a chance of building for himself.

KAIA.

Oh, may he come and thank you for all——

SOLNESS.

[*Harshly.*] I won't have any thanks ! Tell him *that* from me.

KAIA.

Yes, I will——

SOLNESS.

And tell him at the same time that henceforward I don't require his services—nor yours either.

KAIA.

[*Softly and quiveringly.*] Not mine either ?

SOLNESS.

You will have other things to think of now, and to attend to; and that's a very good thing for you. Well, go home with the drawings now, Miss Fosli. Quickly! Do you hear?

KAIA.

[*As before.*] Yes, Mr. Solness.   [*She goes out.*

MRS. SOLNESS.

Heavens! what deceitful eyes she has.

SOLNESS.

She? That poor little creature?

MRS. SOLNESS.

Oh—I can see what I can see, Halvard.——Are you really dismissing them?

SOLNESS.

Yes.

MRS. SOLNESS.

Her as well?

SOLNESS.

Wasn't that what you wished?

L

MRS. SOLNESS.

But how can you get on without *her*—— ? Oh well, no doubt you have some one else in reserve Halvard.

HILDA.

[*Playfully.*] Well, *I* for one am not the person to stand at that desk.

SOLNESS.

Never mind, never mind—it'll be all right, Aline. Now all you have to do is to think about moving into our new home—as quickly as you can. This evening we'll hang up the wreath—[*Turns* to HILDA] —right on the very pinnacle of the tower. What do you say to that, Miss Hilda ?

HILDA.

[*Looks at him with sparkling eyes.*] It'll be splendid to see you so high up once more.

SOLNESS.

Me !

MRS. SOLNESS.

For Heaven's sake, Miss Wangel, don't imagine such a thing ! My husband !—when he always gets so dizzy !

HILDA.

He get dizzy! No, I know quite well he doesn't.

MRS. SOLNESS.

Oh yes, indeed he does.

HILDA.

But I've seen him with my own eyes right up at the top of a high church-tower.

MRS. SOLNESS.

Yes, I hear people talk of that; but it's utterly impossible——

SOLNESS.

[*Vehemently.*] Impossible—impossible, yes! But there I stood all the same!

MRS. SOLNESS.

Oh, how can you say so, Halvard? Why, you can't even bear to go out on the second-storey balcony here. You've always been like that.

SOLNESS.

You may perhaps see something different this evening.

MRS. SOLNESS.

[*In alarm.*] No, no, no! Please God I shall never see that! I'll write at once to the doctor—and I'm sure he won't let you do it.

SOLNESS.

Why Aline——?

MRS. SOLNESS.

Oh, you know you're ill, Halvard. This *proves* it! Oh God—Oh God! [*She goes hastily out to the right.*

HILDA.

[*Looks intently at him.*] Is it so, or is it not?

SOLNESS.

That I turn dizzy?

HILDA.

That *my* master builder *dares* not—*cannot*—climb as high as he builds?

SOLNESS.

Is that the way you look at it?

HILDA.

Yes.

SOLNESS.

I believe there's scarcely a corner in me safe from you.

HILDA.

[*Looks towards the bow-window.*] Up there, then. Right up there——

SOLNESS.

[*Approaches her.*] You might have the topmost chamber in the tower, Hilda—there you might live like a princess.

HILDA.

[*Indefinably, between earnest and jest.*] Yes, that's what you promised me.

SOLNESS.

Did I really?

HILDA.

Fie, Mr. Solness! You said, I should be a princess, and that you would give me a kingdom. And then you went and——Well!

SOLNESS.

[*Cautiously.*] Are you quite certain that this is not a dream-- a fancy, that has fixed itself in your mind?

HILDA.

[*Sharply.*] Do you mean that you didn't do it

SOLNESS.

I scarcely know myself. [*More softly.*] But now I
know *so much* for certain, that I——

HILDA.

That you——? Say it at once!

SOLNESS.

—— that I *ought* to have done it.

HILDA.

[*In a bold outburst.*] Don't tell me *you* can ever be
dizzy!

SOLNESS.

This evening, then, we'll hang up the wreath—
Princess Hilda.

HILDA.

[*With a bitter curve of the lips.*] Over your new
home, yes.

SOLNESS.

Over the new house, which will never be a *home* for
me.   [*He goes out through the garden door.*

HILDA.

[*Looks straight in front of her with a far-away
expression, and whispers to herself. The only words
audible are*] ——frightfully thrilling——

ACT THIRD

A large, broad verandah attached to SOLNESS'S *dwelling-house. Part of the house, with outer door leading to the verandah, is seen to the left. A railing along the verandah to the right. At the back, from the end of the verandah, a flight of steps leads down to the garden below. Tall old trees in the garden spread their branches over the verandah and towards the house. Far to the right, in among the trees, a glimpse is caught of the lower part of the new villa, with scaffolding round so much as is seen of the tower. In the background the garden is bounded by an old wooden fence. Outside the fence, a street with low, tumble-down cottages.*

Evening sky with sun-lit clouds.

On the verandah a garden bench stands along the wall of the house, and in front of the bench a long table. On the other side of the table, an arm-chair and some stools. All the furniture is of wicker-work.

MRS. SOLNESS, *wrapped in a large white crape shawl,
sits resting in the arm-chair and gazes over to the
right. Shortly after,* HILDA WANGEL *comes up the
flight of steps from the garden. She is dressed as
in the last act, and wears her hat. She has in her
bodice a little nosegay of small common flowers.*

MRS. SOLNESS.

[*Turning her head a little.*] Have you been round
the garden, Miss Wangel ?

HILDA.

Yes, I've been taking a look at it.

MRS. SOLNESS.

And found some flowers too, I see.

HILDA.

Yes, indeed.   There are such heaps of them in
among the bushes.

MRS. SOLNESS.

Are there really ?   Still ?   You see I scarcely ever
go there.

HILDA.

[*Closer.*] What !   Don't you take a run down into
the garden every day, then ?

MRS. SOLNESS.

[*With a faint smile.*] I don't "run" anywhere, nowadays.

HILDA.

Well, but don't you go down now and then, to look at all the lovely things there ?

MRS. SOLNESS.

It has all become so strange to me. I'm almost afraid to see it again.

HILDA.

Your own garden !

MRS. SOLNESS.

I don't feel that it is *mine* any longer.

HILDA. .

What do you mean——— ?

MRS. SOLNESS.

No, no, it *is* not—not as it was in my mother's and father's time. They have taken away so much— so much of the garden, Miss Wangel. Fancy—they've parcelled it out--and built houses for strangers— people that I don't know. And *they* can sit and look in upon me from their windows.

HILDA.

[*With a bright expression.*] Mrs. Solness!

MRS SOLNESS.

Yes!

HILDA.

May I stay here with you a little?

MRS SOLNESS.

Yes, by all means, if you care to.

[HILDA *moves a stool close to the arm-chair and
sits down.*

HILDA.

Ah—one can sit here and sun oneself like a cat.

MRS. SOLNESS.

[*Lays her hand softly on* HILDA'S *neck.*] It's nice
of you to be willing to sit with *me*. I thought you
wanted to go in to my husband.

HILDA.

What should I want with him?

MRS. SOLNESS.

To help him, I thought.

HILDA.

No, thanks. And besides, he's not in. He's over there with his workmen. But he looked so fierce that I didn't dare to talk to him.

MRS. SOLNESS.

He's so kind and gentle in reality.

HILDA.

He !

MRS. SOLNESS.

You don't really know him yet, Miss Wangel.

HILDA.

[*Looks affectionately at her.*] Are you pleased at the thought of moving over to the new house ?

MRS. SOLNESS.

I *ought* to be pleased; for it's what Halvard wants——

HILDA.

Oh, not just on that account, surely.

MRS. SOLNESS.

Yes, yes, Miss Wangel; for it's simply my duty to submit myself to *him.* But very often it's dreadfully difficult to force one's mind to obedience.

HILDA.

Yes, *that* must be difficult indeed.

MRS. SOLNESS.

I can tell you it is—when one has so many faults
as I have——

HILDA.

When one has gone through so much as you
have——

MRS. SOLNESS.

How do you know about that?

HILDA.

Your husband told me.

MRS. SOLNESS.

To me he very seldom mentions these things.—Yes,
I can tell you I've gone through more than enough
trouble in my life, Miss Wangel.

HILDA.

[*Looks sympathetically at her and nods slowly.*]
Poor Mrs. Solness. First of all there was the fire——

MRS. SOLNESS.

[*With a sigh.*]   Yes, everything that was *mine* was
burnt.

HILDA.

And then came what was worse.

MRS. SOLNESS.

[*Looking inquiringly at her.*] Worse ?

HILDA.

The worst of all.

MRS. SOLNESS.

What do you mean ?

HILDA.

[*Softly.*] You lost the two little boys.

MRS. SOLNESS.

Oh yes, the boys. But, you see, *that* was a thing apart. That was a dispensation of Providence; and in such things onè can only bow in submission—yes, and be thankful, too.

HILDA.

Then are you so ?

MRS. SOLNESS.

Not always, I'm sorry to say. I know well enough that it's my duty—but all the same I *cannot.*

HILDA.

No, no, I think that's only natural.

MRS. SOLNESS.

And often and often I have to remind myself that it was a righteous punishment for me——

HILDA.

Why?

MRS. SOLNESS.

Because I hadn't fortitude enough in misfortune.

HILDA.

But I don't see that——

MRS. SOLNESS.

Oh, no, no, Miss Wangel—don't talk to me any more about the two little boys. We ought to feel nothing but joy in thinking of *them ;* for they are so happy—so happy now. No, it's the *small* losses in life that cut one to the heart—the loss of all that other people look upon as almost nothing.

HILDA.

[*Lays her arms on* MRS. SOLNESS' *knees and looks up at her affectionately.*] Dear Mrs. Solness—tell me what things you mean!

MRS. SOLNESS.

As I say, only little things. All the old portraits were burnt on the walls. And all the old silk dresses were burnt, that had belonged to the family for generations and generations. And all mother's and grandmother's lace — that was burnt, too. And only think—the jewels, too ! [*Sadly.*] And then all the dolls.

HILDA.

The dolls ?

MRS. SOLNESS.

[*Choking with tears.*] I had nine lovely dolls.

HILDA.

And *they* were burnt too ?

MRS. SOLNESS.

All of them. Oh, it was hard—so hard for me.

HILDA.

Had you put by all these dolls, then ? Ever since you were little ?

MRS. SOLNESS.

I hadn't put them by. The dolls and I had gone on living together.

HILDA.

After you were grown up ?

MRS. SOLNESS.

Yes, long after that.

HILDA.

After you were married, too ?

MRS. SOLNESS.

Oh yes, indeed. So long as he didn't see it——.
But they were all burnt up, poor things. No one
thought of saving them. Oh, it's so miserable to
think of. You mustn't laugh at me, Miss Wangel.

HILDA.

I'm not laughing in the least.

MRS. SOLNESS.

For you see, in a certain sense, there was life in
them, too. I carried them under my heart—like
little unborn children.

[DR. HERDAL, *with his hat in his hand, comes
out through the door and observes* MRS.
SOLNESS *and* HILDA.

DR. HERDAL.

Well, Mrs. Solness, so you're sitting out here catching cold?

MRS. SOLNESS.

I find it so pleasant and warm here to-day.

DR. HERDAL.

Yes, yes. But is there anything going on here? I got a note from you.

MRS. SOLNESS.

[*Rises.*] Yes, there's something I must talk to you about.

DR. HERDAL.

Very well; then perhaps we'd better go in. [*To* HILDA.] Still in your mountaineering dress, Miss Wangel?

HILDA.

[*Gaily, rising.*] Yes—in full uniform! But to-day I'm not going climbing and breaking my neck. We two will stop quietly below and look on, doctor.

DR. HERDAL.

What are we to look on at?

M

MRS. SOLNESS.

[*Softly, in alarm, to* HILDA.] Hush, hush—for God's sake! He's coming! Try to get that idea out of his head. And let us be friends, Miss Wangel. Don't you think we can?

HILDA.

[*Throws her arms impetuously round* MRS. SOLNESS'S *neck.*] Oh, if we only could!

MRS. SOLNESS.

[*Gently disengages herself.*] There, there, there! There he comes, doctor. Let me have a word with you.

DR. HERDAL.

Is it about *him?*

MRS. SOLNESS.

Yes, to be sure it's about him. Do come in.

> [*She and the doctor enter the house. Next moment* SOLNESS *comes up from the garden by the flight of steps. A serious look comes over* HILDA'S *face.*

SOLNESS.

[*Glances at the house-door, which is closed cautiously from within.*] Have you noticed, Hilda, that as soon as I come, she goes?

HILDA.

I've noticed that as soon as you come, you make her go.

SOLNESS.

Perhaps so. But I cannot help it. [*Looks observantly at her.*] Are you cold, Hilda? I think you look so.

HILDA.

I've just come up out of a tomb.

SOLNESS.

What do you mean by *that?*

HILDA.

That I've got chilled through and through, Mr. Solness.

SOLNESS.

[*Slowly.*] I believe I understand——

HILDA.

What brings you up here just now?

SOLNESS.

I caught sight of you from over there.

HILDA.

But then you must have seen her too?

SOLNESS.

I knew she would go at once if I came.

HILDA.

Is it very painful for you that she should avoid you in this way?

SOLNESS.

In one sense, it's a relief as well.

HILDA.

Not to have her before your eyes?

SOLNESS.

Yes.

HILDA.

Not to be always seeing how heavily the loss of the little boys weighs upon her?

SOLNESS.

Yes. Chiefly that.

> [HILDA *drifts across the verandah with her hands behind her back, stops at the railing and looks out over the garden.*

SOLNESS.

[*After a short pause.*] Did you have a long talk with her ?

[HILDA *stands motionless and does not answer.*

SOLNESS.

Had you a long talk, I asked ?

[HILDA *is silent as before.*

SOLNESS.

What was she talking about, Hilda ?

[HILDA *continues silent.*

SOLNESS.

Poor Aline ! I suppose it was about the little boys.

HILDA.

[*A nervous shudder runs through her ; then she nods hurriedly once or twice.*]

SOLNESS.

She will never get over it—never in this world. [*Approaches her.*] Now you're standing there again like a statue ; just as you stood last night.

HILDA.

[*Turns and looks at him with great serious eyes.*] I am going away.

SOLNESS.

[*Sharply.*] Going away !

HILDA.

Yes.

SOLNESS.

But I won't allow you to.

HILDA.

What am I to do *here* now ?

SOLNESS.

Simply to *be* here, Hilda !

HILDA.

[*Measures him with a look.*] Oh, thank you. You know it wouldn't end there.

SOLNESS.

[*Without consideration.*] So much the better.

HILDA.

[*Vehemently.*] I *can't* do any harm to one I *know !* I can't take away anything that belongs to her.

SOLNESS.

Who wants you to do that?

HILDA.

[*Continuing.*] A stranger, yes! for that's quite a different thing. A person I've never set eyes on. But one that I've come into close contact with——! No! oh no! Ugh!

SOLNESS.

Yes, but I never proposed you should.

HILDA.

Oh, Mr. Solness, you know quite well what the end of it would be. And that's why I'm going away.

SOLNESS.

And what's to become of me when you're gone? What shall I have to live for *then ?*—After that?

HILDA.

[*With the indefinable look in her eyes.*] It's surely not so hard for *you.* You have your duties to her. Live for those duties.

SOLNESS.

Too late. These powers—these—these——

HILDA.

——devils——

SOLNESS.

Yes, these devils! And the troll within me as well—
they have drawn all the life-blood out of her. [*Laughs
in desperation.*] They did it for my *happiness.* Yes,
yes! [*Sadly.*] And now she's dead—for my sake.
And I am chained alive to a dead woman. [*In wild
anguish.*] I—I who *cannot* live without joy in life!

> [HILDA *walks round the table and seats herself
> on the bench with her elbows on the table,
> and her head supported by her hands.*

HILDA.

[*Sits and looks at him awhile.*] What will you build˙
next?

SOLNESS.

[*Shakes his head.*] I don't believe I shall build much
more.

HILDA.

Not those cosy, happy homes for mother and father,
and for the troop of children?

SOLNESS.

I wonder whether there will be any use for such
homes in the times that are coming.

HILDA.

Poor Mr. Solness! And you have gone all these ten years—and staked your whole life—on that alone.

SOLNESS.

Yes, you may well say so, Hilda.

HILDA.

[*With an outburst.*] Oh, it all seems to me so foolish —so foolish!

SOLNESS.

All what?

HILDA.

Not to be able to grasp at your own happiness—at your own life! Merely because some one you know happens to stand in the way!

SOLNESS.

One whom you have no right to set aside.

HILDA.

I wonder whether one really *hasn't* the right? And yet, and yet——. Oh! if one could only sleep the whole thing away!

> [*She lays her arms flat down on the table, rests the left side of her head on her hands and shuts her eyes.*

SOLNESS.

[*Turns the arm-chair and sits down at the table.*] Had *you* a cosy, happy home—up with your father, Hilda?

HILDA.

[*Without stirring, answers as if half asleep.*] I had only a cage.

SOLNESS.

And you're determined not to return to it?

HILDA.

[*As before.*] The wild bird never wants to go into the cage.

SOLNESS.

Rather range through the free air——

HILDA.

[*Still as before.*] The bird of prey loves to range——

SOLNESS.

[*Lets his eyes rest on her.*] If only one had the viking-spirit in life——

HILDA.

[*In her usual voice; opens her eyes but does not move.*] And the other thing? Say what *that* was!

SOLNESS.

A robust conscience.

[HILDA *sits up on the bench with animation.
Her eyes have once more the sparkling
expression of gladness.*

HILDA.

[*Nods to him.*] *I* know what you're going to build
next!

SOLNESS.

Then you know more than I do, Hilda.

HILDA.

Yes, builders are such stupid people.

SOLNESS.

What is it to be then?

HILDA.

[*Nods again.*] The castle.

SOLNESS.

What castle?

HILDA.

My castle, of course.

SOLNESS.

Do you want a castle now ?

HILDA.

Don't you owe me a kingdom, I'd like to know ?

SOLNESS.

You say I do.

HILDA.

Well—you admit you owe me this kingdom. And you can't have a kingdom without a royal castle, I should think !

SOLNESS.

[*More and more animated.*] Yes, they usually go together.

HILDA.

Good ! Then build it for me this moment ?

SOLNESS

[*Laughing.*] Must you have that on the instant, too ?

HILDA.

Yes, to be sure ! For the ten years are up now, and I'm not going to wait any longer. So—out with the castle, Mr. Solness !

SOLNESS.

It's no light matter to owe you anything, Hilda.

HILDA.

You should have thought of that before. It's too late now. So—[*tapping the table*]—the castle on the table! It's *my* castle. I will have it *at once!*

SOLNESS.

[*More seriously, leans over towards her, with his arms on the table.*] What sort of castle have you imagined, Hilda?

[*Her expression becomes more and more veiled. She seems gazing inwards at herself.*

HILDA.

[*Slowly.*] My castle shall stand on a height—on a very great height—with a clear outlook on all sides, so that I can see far—far around.

SOLNESS.

And no doubt it's to have a high tower?

HILDA.

A tremendously high tower. And at the very top of the tower there shall be a balcony. And I will stand out upon it——

SOLNESS.

[*Involuntarily clutches at his forehead.*] How can you like to stand at such a dizzy height—— ?

HILDA.

Yes, I will! Right up there will I stand and look down on the other people—on those that are building churches, and homes for mother and father and the troop of children. And *you* may come up and look on at it, too.

SOLNESS.

[*In a low tone.*] Is the builder to be allowed to come up beside the princess ?

HILDA.

If the builder *will.*

SOLNESS.

[*More softly.*] Then I think the builder will come.

HILDA.

[*Nods.*] The builder—he'll come.

SOLNESS.

But he'll never be able to build any more. Poor builder !

HILDA.

[*Animated.*] Oh yes, he will! We two will set to work together. And then we'll build the loveliest— the very loveliest—thing in all the world.

SOLNESS.

[*Intently.*] Hilda, tell me what that is!

HILDA.

[*Looks smilingly at him, shakes her head a little, pouts, and speaks as if to a child.*] Builders—they are such very—very stupid people.

SOLNESS.

Yes, no doubt they're stupid. But now tell me what it is—the loveliest thing in the world—that we two are to build together?

HILDA.

[*Is silent a little while, then says with an indefinable expression in her eyes.*] Castles in the air.

SOLNESS.

Castles in the air?

HILDA.

[*Nods.*] Castles in the air, yes! Do you know what sort of thing a castle in the air is?

SOLNESS.

It's the loveliest thing in the world, you say.

HILDA.

[*Rises with vehemence, and makes a gesture of repulsion with her hand.*] Yes, to be sure it is! Castles in the air—they're so easy to take refuge in. And so easy to build, too—[*looks scornfully at him*]—especially for the builders who have a—a dizzy conscience.

SOLNESS.

[*Rises.*] After this day we two will build together, Hilda.

HILDA.

[*With a half-dubious smile.*] A *real* castle in the air?

SOLNESS.

Yes. One with a firm foundation under it.

RAGNAR BROVIK *comes out from the house. He is carrying a large, green wreath with flowers and silken ribbons.*

HILDA.

[*With an outburst of pleasure.*] The wreath! Oh, that'll be glorious!

SOLNESS.

[*In surprise.*] Have *you* brought the wreath, Ragnar ?

RAGNAR.

I promised the foreman I would.

SOLNESS.

[*Relieved.*] Ah, then I suppose your father's better ?

RAGNAR.

No.

SOLNESS.

Wasn't he cheered by what I wrote ?

RAGNAR.

It came too late.

SOLNESS.

Too late !

RAGNAR.

When she came with it, he was unconscious. He had had a stroke.

SOLNESS.

Why, then, you must go home to him ! You must attend to your father !

N

RAGNAR.

He doesn't need me any more.

SOLNESS.

But surely you ought to be with him.

RAGNAR.

She is sitting by his bed.

SOLNESS.

[*Rather uncertainly.*] Kaia?

RAGNAR.

[*Looking darkly at him.*] Yes—Kaia.

SOLNESS.

Go home, Ragnar—both to him and to her. Give *me* the wreath.

RAGNAR.

[*Suppresses a mocking smile.*] You don't mean that you yourself—— ?

SOLNESS.

I will take it down to them myself. [*Takes the wreath from him.*] And now, you go home; we don't require you to·day.

RAGNAR.

I know you don't require me any more; but to-day
I shall stop.

SOLNESS.

Well, stop then, since you're bent upon it.

HILDA.

[*At the railing.*] Mr. Solness, I will stand here
and look on at you. .

SOLNESS.

At me!

HILDA.

It will be fearfully thrilling.

SOLNESS.

[*In a low tone.*] We'll talk about that another time,
Hilda.

> [*He goes down the flight of steps with the wreath,
> and away through the garden.*

HILDA.

[*Looks after him, then turns to* RAGNAR.] You might
at least have thanked him, I think.

RAGNAR.

Thanked him ? Ought I to have thanked *him* ?

HILDA.

Yes, of course you ought !

RAGNAR.

I think it's rather you I ought to thank.

HILDA.

How can you say such a thing ?

RAGNAR.

[*Without answering her.*] But I advise you to take care, Miss Wangel ! For you don't know *him* rightly yet.

HILDA.

[*Ardently.*] Oh, I know him better than any one !

RAGNAR.

[*Laughs in exasperation.*] Thank him, when he's held me down year after year ! When he made father disbelieve in me—made me disbelieve in myself ! And all merely that he might—— !

HILDA.

[*As if divining something.*] That he might——? Tell me at once !

RAGNAR.

That he might keep her with him.

HILDA.

[*With a start towards him.*] The girl at the desk!

RAGNAR.

Yes.

HILDA.

[*Threateningly, clenching her hands.*] That is not true! You're telling falsehoods about him!

RAGNAR.

I wouldn't believe it either until to-day—when she said so herself.

HILDA.

[*As if beside herself.*] *What* did she say? I *will* know! At once! at once!

RAGNAR.

She said that he had taken possession of her mind—her whole mind—centred all her thoughts upon himself alone. She says that she can never leave him—that she will remain here, where *he* is——

HILDA.

[*With flashing eyes.*] She won't be allowed to!

RAGNAR.

[*As if feeling his way.*] Who won't allow her?

HILDA.

[*Rapidly.*] *He* won't either?

RAGNAR.

Oh no—I understand the whole thing now. After this she would merely be—in the way.

HILDA.

You understand nothing—since you can talk like that! No, *I* will tell you why he kept hold of her.

RAGNAR.

Well then, why?

HILDA.

In order to keep hold of *you*.

RAGNAR.

Has he told you so?

HILDA.

No, but it is so. It *must* be so! [*Wildly.*] I will—
I *will* have it so!

RAGNAR.

And at the very moment when you came—he let
her go.

HILDA.

It was *you—you* that he let go? What do you
suppose he cares about strange women like her?

RAGNAR.

[*Reflects.*] Is it possible that all this time he's been
afraid of me?

HILDA.

He afraid! I wouldn't be so conceited if I were
you.

RAGNAR.

Oh, he must have seen long ago that I had something in me, too. Besides—cowardly—that's just
what he is, you see.

HILDA.

He! Oh yes, I'm likely to believe *that*.

RAGNAR.

In a certain sense he *is* cowardly—he, the great master builder. He's not afraid of robbing others of their life's happiness—as he has done both for my father and for me. But when it comes to climbing a paltry bit of scaffolding—he'll do anything rather than *that*.

HILDA.

Oh, you should just have seen him high, high up— at the dizzy height where I once saw him.

RAGNAR.

Did you see that?

HILDA.

Yes, indeed I did. How free and great he looked as he stood and fastened the wreath to the church-vane!

RAGNAR.

I know that he ventured that, *once* in his life—one solitary time. It's a tradition among us younger men. But no power on earth would induce him to do it again.

HILDA.

To-day he will do it again!

RAGNAR.

[*Scornfully.*] Yes, I daresay!

HILDA.

We shall see it.

RAGNAR.

That neither you nor I will see.

HILDA.

[*With uncontrollable vehemence.*] I *will* see it! I *will* and I *must* see it!

RAGNAR.

But he won't do it. He simply daren't do it. For you see he can't get over this infirmity—master builder though he be.

MRS. SOLNESS *comes from the house on to the verandah.*

MRS. SOLNESS.

[*Looks around.*] Isn't he here? Where has he gone to?

RAGNAR.

Mr. Solness is down with the men.

HILDA.

He took the wreath with him.

MRS. SOLNESS.

[*Terrified.*] Took the wreath with him! Oh God! oh God! Brovik—you must go down to him! Get him to come back here!

RAGNAR.

Shall I say you want to speak to him, Mrs. Solness?

MRS. SOLNESS.

Oh yes, do! No, no—don't say that *I* want anything! You can say that somebody is here, and that he must come at once.

RAGNAR.

Good. I will do so, Mrs. Solness.

[*He goes down the flight of steps and away through the garden.*

MRS. SOLNESS.

Oh, Miss Wangel, you can't think how anxious I feel about him.

HILDA.

Is there anything in this to be so terribly frightened about?

MRS. SOLNESS.

Oh yes; surely you can understand. Just think, if he were really to do it! If he should take it into his head to climb up the scaffolding!

HILDA.

[*Eagerly.*] Do you think he will?

MRS. SOLNESS.

Oh, one can never tell what he might take into his head. I'm afraid there's nothing he mightn't think of doing.

HILDA.

Aha! Perhaps you too think that he's—well——?

MRS. SOLNESS.

Oh, I don't know what to think about him now. The doctor has been telling me all sorts of things; and putting it all together with several things I've heard him say——

Dr. Herdal *looks out through the door.*

Dr. Herdal.

Isn't he coming soon ?

Mrs. Solness.

Yes, I think so.   I've sent for him at any rate.

Dr. Herdal.

[*Coming closer.*] I'm afraid you'll have to go in, my dear lady——

Mrs. Solness.

Oh no !   Oh no !   I shall stay out here and wait for Halvard.

Dr. Herdal.

But some ladies have just come to call on you——

Mrs. Solness.

Good heavens, that too ! And just at this moment !

Dr. Herdal.

They say they positively must see the ceremony.

MRS. SOLNESS.

Well, well, I suppose I must go to them after all. It's my duty.

HILDA.

Can't you ask the ladies to go away ?

MRS. SOLNESS.

No that would never do.   Now that they're here, it's my duty to see them.   But do you stay out here in the meantime, and receive him when he comes.

DR. HERDAL.

And try to occupy his attention as long as possible——

MRS. SOLNESS.

Yes, do, dear Miss Wangel.   Keep as firm hold of him as ever you can.

HILDA

Wouldn't it be best for you to do that ?

MRS. SOLNESS.

Yes ; God knows that is *my* duty.   But when one has duties in so many directions——

DR. HERDAL.

[*Looks towards the garden.*] There he's coming !

MRS. SOLNESS.

And I have to go in !

DR. HERDAL.

[*To* HILDA.] Don't say anything about *my* being here.

HILDA.

Oh no ! I daresay I shall find something else to talk to Mr. Solness about.

MRS. SOLNESS.

And be sure you keep firm hold of him. I believe *you* can do it best.

> [MRS. SOLNESS *and* DR. HERDAL *go into the house.* HILDA *remains standing on the verandah.* SOLNESS *comes from the garden, up the flight of steps.*

SOLNESS.

Somebody wants me, I hear.

HILDA.

Yes ; it's I, Mr. Solness.

SOLNESS.

Oh, is it you, Hilda? I was afraid it might be Aline or the Doctor.

HILDA.

You're very easily frightened, it seems!

SOLNESS.

Do you think so?

HILDA.

Yes; people say that you're afraid to climb about— on the scaffoldings, you know.

SOLNESS.

Well, that's quite a special thing.

HILDA.

Then it's true that you're afraid to do it.

SOLNESS.

Yes, I am.

HILDA.

Afraid of falling down and killing yourself?

SOLNESS.

No, not of that.

HILDA.

Of what, then?

SOLNESS.

I'm afraid of retribution, Hilda.

HILDA.

Of retribution ? [*Shakes her head.*] I don't understand that.

SOLNESS.

Sit down, and I'll tell you something.

HILDA.

Yes, do—at once !

> [*She sits on a stool by the railing, and looks
> expectantly at him.*

SOLNESS.

[*Throws his hat on the table.*] You know that I
began by building churches.

HILDA.

[*Nods.*] I know that well.

SOLNESS.

For, you see, I came as a boy from a pious home
in the country; and so it seemed to me that this church-
building was the noblest task I could set myself.

HILDA.

Yes, yes.

SOLNESS.

And I venture to say that I built those poor little churches with such honest and warm and heart-felt devotion that—that——

HILDA.

That——? Well?

SOLNESS.

Well, that I think he ought to have been pleased with me.

HILDA.

He? What *he?*

SOLNESS.

He who was to have the churches, of course! He to whose honour and glory they were dedicated. ·

HILDA.

Oh, indeed! But are you certain, then, that—that he wasn't—pleased with you?

SOLNESS.

[*Scornfully.*] *He* pleased with *me!* How can you talk so, Hilda? He who gave the troll in me leave to lord it just as it pleased. He who bade them be at hand to serve me, both day and night—all these—all these——

o

HILDA.

Devils——

SOLNESS.

Yes, of both kinds. Oh no, he made me feel clearly enough that he wasn't pleased with me. [*Mysteriously.*] You see, that was really the reason why he made the old house burn down.

HILDA.

Was that why?

SOLNESS.

Yes, don't you understand? He wanted to give me the chance of becoming an accomplished master in my own sphere—so that I might build all the more glorious churches for him. At first I didn't understand what he was driving at; but all of a sudden it flashed upon me.

HILDA.

When was that?

SOLNESS.

It was when I was building the church-tower up at Lysanger.

HILDA.

I thought so.

SOLNESS.

For you see, Hilda—up there, amid those new sur-roundings, I used to go about musing and pondering within myself. Then I saw plainly why he had taken my little children from me. It was that I should have nothing else to attach myself to. No such thing as love and happiness, you understand. I was to be only a master builder—nothing else. And all my life long I was to go on building for him. [*Laughs.*] But I can tell you nothing came of that.

HILDA.

What did you do, then ?

SOLNESS.

First of all, I searched and tried my own heart——

HILDA.

And then ?

SOLNESS.

Then I did the *impossible*—I no less than *he*.

HILDA.

The impossible ?

SOLNESS.

I had never before been able to climb up to a great, free height. But that day I did it.

HILDA.

[*Leaping up.*] Yes, yes, you did !

SOLNESS.

And when I stood there, high over everything, and
was hanging the wreath over the vane, I said to him :
Hear me now, thou Mighty One! From this day
forward I will be a free builder—I too, in my sphere—
just as thou in thine. I will never build any more
churches for thee—only homes for human beings.

HILDA.

[*With great sparkling eyes.*] *That* was the song that
I heard through the air !

SOLNESS.

But afterwards his turn came.

HILDA.

What do you mean ?

SOLNESS.

[*Looks disconsolately at her.*] Building homes for
human beings is not worth sixpence, Hilda.

HILDA.

Do you say *that* now ?

SOLNESS.

Yes, for now I *see* it. Men have no use for these homes of theirs—to be happy in. And I shouldn't have had any use for such a home, if I'd had one. [*With a quiet, bitter laugh.*] See, that is the upshot of the whole affair, however far back I look. Nothing really built; nor anything sacrificed for the chance of building. Nothing, nothing! the whole is nothing!

HILDA.

Then you will never build anything more?

SOLNESS.

[*With animation.*] On the contrary, I'm just going to begin.

HILDA.

What, then? What will you build? Tell me at once!

SOLNESS.

I believe there's only one possible dwelling-place for human happiness—and that's what I'm going to build now.

HILDA.

[*Looks firmly at him.*] Mr. Solness—you mean our castles in the air.

SOLNESS.

The castles in the air—yes.

HILDA.

I'm afraid you would turn dizzy before we got half-way up.

SOLNESS.

Not if I can mount hand in hand with you, Hilda.

HILDA.

[*With an expression of suppressed resentment.*] Only with me? Won't there be others of the party?

SOLNESS.

Who else should there be?

HILDA.

Oh—that girl—that Kaia at the desk. Poor thing — don't you want to take her with you too?

SOLNESS.

Oho! Was it about her that Aline was talking to you?

HILDA.

Is it so—yes or no?

SOLNESS.

[*Vehemently.*] I won't answer such a question! You must believe in me, utterly and entirely !

HILDA.

All these ten years I've believed in you so fully— so fully.

SOLNESS.

You must go on believing in me !

HILDA.

Then let me see you stand free and high up !

SOLNESS.

[*Sadly.*] Oh Hilda—it's not every day that I can do that.

HILDA.

[*Passionately.*] I will have you do it ! I will have it ! [*Imploringly.*] Just once more, Mr. Solness ! Do the *impossible* once again !

SOLNESS.

[*Stands and looks deep into her eyes.*] *If* I try it, Hilda, I will stand up there and talk to him as I did that time before.

HILDA.

[*In rising excitement.*] What will you say to him?

SOLNESS.

I will say to him : Hear me, Mighty Lord—thou may'st judge me as seems best to thee. But hereafter I will build nothing but the loveliest thing in the world——

HILDA.

[*Carried away.*] Yes—yes—yes!

SOLNESS.

—build it together with a princess, whom I love——

HILDA.

Yes, tell him that! Tell him that!

SOLNESS.

Yes. And then I will say to him : Now I shall go down and throw my arms round her and kiss her——

HILDA.

—many times! Say that!

SOLNESS.

—many, many times, I will say.

HILDA.

And then—— ?

SOLNESS.

Then I will wave my hat—and come down to the earth—and do as I said to him.

HILDA.

[*With outstretched arms.*] Now I see you again as I did when there was song in the air !

SOLNESS.

[*Looks at her with his head bowed.*] How have you become what you are, Hilda ?

HILDA.

How have you made me what I am ?

SOLNESS.

[*Shortly and firmly.*] The princess shall have her castle.

HILDA.

[*Jubilant, clapping her hands.*] Oh, Mr. Solness—— ! My lovely, lovely castle.   Our castle in the air !

SOLNESS.

On a firm foundation.

> [*In the street a crowd of people has assembled, vaguely seen through the trees. Music of wind-instruments is heard far away behind the new house*

[MRS. SOLNESS, *with a fur collar round her neck*, DOCTOR HERDAL *with her white shawl on his arm, and some ladies, come out on the verandah.* RAGNAR BROVIK *comes at the same time up from the garden.*

MRS. SOLNESS.

[*To* RAGNAR.] Are we to have music, too?

RAGNAR.

Yes. It's the band of the Masons' Union. [*To* SOLNESS.] The foreman asked me to tell you that he's ready now to go up with the wreath.

SOLNESS.

[*Takes his hat.*] All right. I'll go down to him myself.

MRS. SOLNESS.

[*Anxiously.*] What have you to do down there, Halvard?

SOLNESS.

[*Curtly.*] I must be down below with the men.

MRS. SOLNESS.

Yes, down below—only down below.

SOLNESS.

That's where I always stand—on everyday occasions.

[*He goes down the flight of steps and away through the garden.*

MRS. SOLNESS.

[*Calls after him over the railing.*] But do beg the man to be careful when he goes up! Promise me that, Halvard!

DR. HERDAL.

[*To* MRS. SOLNESS.] Don't you see that I was right? He's given up all thought of that folly.

MRS. SOLNESS.

Oh, what a relief! Twice workmen have fallen, and each time they were killed on the spot. [*Turns to* HILDA.] Thank you, Miss Wangel, for having kept such a firm hold upon him. I should never have had my own way with him.

DR. HERDAL.

[*Playfully.*] Yes, yes, Miss Wangel, you know how to keep firm hold on a man, when you give your mind to it.

> [MRS. SOLNESS *and* DR. HERDAL *go up to the ladies, who are standing nearer to the steps and looking over the garden.* HILDA *remains standing beside the railing in the foreground.* RAGNAR *goes up to her.*

RAGNAR.

[*With suppressed laughter, half whispering.*] Miss Wangel, do you see all those young fellows down in the street?

HILDA

Yes.

RAGNAR.

They're my fellow-students come to look at the master.

HILDA.

What do they want to look at *him* for?

RAGNAR.

They want to see how he daren't climb to the top of his own house.

HILDA.

Oh, *that's* what those boys want, is it ?

RAGNAR.

[*Spitefully and scornfully.*] He's kept us down so long, that man. Now we're going to see him keep quietly down below himself.

HILDA.

You won't see that—not this time.

RAGNAR.

[*Smiles.*] Indeed! Then where shall we see him ?

HILDA.

High—high up by the vane! That's where you'll see him !

RAGNAR.

[*Laughs.*] Him! Oh yes, I daresay !

HILDA.

His *will* is to reach the top—so at the top you shall see him.

RAGNAR.

His *will*, yes; that I can easily believe. But he simply *can't* do it. His head would swim round, long, long before he got half-way. He'd have to crawl down again on his hands and knees.

DR. HERDAL.

[*Points across.*] Look! there goes the foreman up the ladders.

MRS. SOLNESS.

And of course he's got the wreath to carry too. Oh, I do hope he'll be careful!

RAGNAR.

[*Stares incredulously and shouts.*] Why, but it's——

HILDA.

[*Breaking out in jubilation.*] It's the master builder himself?

MRS. SOLNESS.

[*Screams with terror.*] Yes, it's Halvard! Oh my great God——! Halvard! Halvard!

DR. HERDAL.

Hush! Don't shout to him!

MRS. SOLNESS.

[*Half beside herself.*] I must go to him! I must bring him down again.

DR. HERDAL.

[*Holds her.*] Don't move, any of you! Not a sound!

HILDA.

[*Immovable, follows* SOLNESS *with her eyes.*] He climbs and climbs. Higher and higher! Higher and higher! Look! Just look!

RAGNAR.

[*Breathless.*] He *must* turn now. He can't possibly help it.

HILDA.

He climbs and climbs. He'll soon be at the top now.

MRS. SOLNESS

Oh, I shall die of terror. I can't bear to see it!

DR. HERDAL.

Then don't look up at him.

HILDA.

There, he's standing on the topmost planks! Right at the top!

DR. HERDAL.

Nobody must move! Do you hear?

HILDA.

[*Exulting, with quiet intensity.*] At last ! At last !
Now I see him great and free again !

RAGNAR.

[*Almost voiceless.*] But this is im——

HILDA.

So I have seen him all through these ten years.
How secure he stands ! Frightfully thrilling all the
same. Look at him ! Now he's hanging the
wreath round the vane !

RAGNAR.

I feel as if I were looking at something utterly
impossible.

HILDA.

Yes, it *is* the *impossible* that he's doing now !
[*With the indefinable expression in her eyes.*] Can
you see any one else up there with him ?

RAGNAR.

There is no one else.

HILDA.

Yes, there is one he is striving with.

RAGNAR.

You are mistaken.

HILDA.

Then do you hear no song in the air, either ?

RAGNAR.

It must be the wind in the tree-tops.

HILDA.

I hear a song—a mighty song! [*Shouts in wild jubilation and glee.*] Look, look ! Now he's waving his hat ! He's waving it to us down here ! Oh, wave, wave back to him ! For now it's finished ! [*Tears the white shawl from the Doctor, waves it, and shouts up to* SOLNESS.] Hurrah for Master Builder Solness !

DR. HERDAL.

Stop ! Stop ! For God's sake—— !

> [*The ladies on the verandah wave their pocket-
> handkerchiefs, and the shouts of "Hurrah"
> are taken up in the street below. Then they
> are suddenly silenced, and the crowd bursts
> out into a shriek of horror. A human
> body, with planks and fragments of wood,
> is vaguely perceived crashing down behind
> the trees.*

P

MRS. SOLNESS AND THE LADIES.

[*At the same time.*] He's falling! He's falling!

[MRS. SOLNESS *totters, falls backwards, swoon-*
ing, and is caught, amid cries and con-
fusion, by the ladies. The crowd in the
street breaks down the fence and storms into
the garden. At the same time DR. HERDAL,
too, rushes down thither. A short pause.

HILDA.

[*Stares fixedly upwards, and says, as if petrified :*]
My Master Builder.

RAGNAR.

[*Supports himself, trembling, against the railing.*]
He must be dashed to pieces—killed on the spot.

ONE OF THE LADIES.

[*Whilst* MRS. SOLNESS *is carried into the house.*] Run
down for the doctor——

RAGNAR.

I can't stir a foot——

ANOTHER LADY.

Then call to some one!

RAGNAR.

[*Tries to call out.*] How is it?   Is he alive?

A VOICE.

[*Below, in the garden.*] Mr. Solness is dead ! ·

OTHER VOICES.

[*Nearer.*] The head is all crushed.—He fell right into the quarry.

HILDA.

[*Turns to* RAGNAR, *and says quietly.*] I can't see him up there now.

RAGNAR.

This is terrible. So, after all, he could not do it.

HILDA.

[*As if in quiet spell-bound triumph.*] But he mounted right to the top. And I heard harps in the air. [*Waves her shawl in the air, and shrieks with wild intensity.*] *My—my* Master Builder !

CPSIA information can be obtained at www.ICGtesting.com
Printed in the USA
LVOW131616210613

339728LV00002B/234/P